COOKING FOR YOUR
BABY AND TODDLER

COOKING FOR YOUR
BABY AND TODDLER

Louise Fulton Keats

hardie grant books
MELBOURNE · LONDON

DEDICATION

To my boys, John and Harry.

ACKNOWLEDGEMENTS

I could not have written this book without the knowledge and expertise of so many people. My most heartfelt thanks to Dr Peter Campbell, neonatologist and paediatrician, and Kay Gibbons, dietitian at The Royal Children's Hospital Melbourne, both of whom reviewed and provided extensive feedback on the text. I am also indebted to paediatric gastroenterologist, Dr Reuben Jackson, for giving so generously of his time to walk me through some of the finer medical details of infant feeding. Thanks also to Dr Gie Liem of Deakin University for sharing his expertise on children's taste preferences. And thanks to dietitian Glenn Cardwell for being such a helpful sounding board (for those interested, his online nutrition newsletter is an excellent read). Thanks also to health and fitness guru, Amelia Burton, for her fascinating and entertaining insights, and her support throughout this project. And thanks to those at the National Health and Medical Research Council, Food Standards Australia New Zealand, and the NSW Food Authority who assisted so graciously with my numerous requests for information.

My gratitude also goes to the great many parents I interviewed for this book. Your insights played a significant role in shaping the book's content and opened my eyes to just how many different, wonderful approaches one can take to feeding a family.

A huge thank you to the amazing team behind the food photography, who all put in a superhuman effort during our intense photo shoot. Thanks to Ben Dearnley, whose photography is nothing short of magical, and to Michelle Noerianto, for her absolutely stunning styling. Thanks also to Kerrie Ray, for her extraordinary energy and perfect cooking, and to my mum, Suzanne Gibbs, who worked tirelessly behind the scenes during the shoot. It's pretty extraordinary to have one of Australia's finest food writers as a sous chef! Thanks also to Zoë Hart and Sean Beavis, who so generously made available their beautiful home for the shoot. I am blessed to have such good friends.

My sincere thanks also to all the team at Hardie Grant for this wonderful opportunity. Thanks to Justine Harding, for her fine editing and for handling my endless requests with such good humour, and to Lucy Heaver, for her boundless enthusiasm, patience and wisdom. Thanks also to Gordana Trifunovic for her early work on the project. And particular thanks to my publisher, Paul McNally, whose influence has changed my life these past two years.

Finally, to my wonderful family, John, Harry, Mum, Dad, Kate and Grandma. You are my raison d'être. Thank you for supporting me during this all-consuming project. Your patience, encouragement and love have meant more to me than you can imagine.

CONTENTS

INTRODUCTION

It wasn't until I started school that I realised my sister and I were a bit different from most kids. While other children had peanut butter sandwiches in their lunchboxes, ours were filled with frittatas, dolmades and roasted vegetables. Although I adored Mum's cooking, this used to cause me serious embarrassment. Why couldn't I have white-bread sandwiches like everyone else? But, when you come from a culinary household, that isn't an option. Both my mum and grandma are food writers, so my childhood was filled with recipe testing and attempts at recreating the dishes they'd tried on their many food adventures. As an adult, I'm now eternally grateful for the extraordinary world of food I grew up in. By teaching me to cook and to have a love of different cuisines, Mum and Grandma knew that I would eat well for the rest of my life.

Now that I have a child of my own, my great hope is that I will be able to nurture in him the love of food that my family gave to me. While there is an element of luck involved and some children are inherently more adventurous eaters than others, I have learned through my research in childhood nutrition that, as a parent, I have extraordinary influence over shaping my son's palate and his willingness to eat different foods. Scientists have done a mountain of work in this area and we now know that the vast majority of taste preferences are learned over time, depending on exposure.

With this in mind, from the time I started my son on solids I have made it my mission to make his food experiences as varied as possible. This doesn't mean spending hours at the stove cooking apple four ways – like every mum, I don't have time for that. It just means that I sometimes buy a pomegranate or lychee and give him a try. It means that if he's had orange for breakfast one day, I'll give him kiwifruit the next. It means I won't give him peas every night of the week. Instead, he'll have broccoli, chickpeas and beetroot. It means offering him tomato yet again, even if he's turned his nose up at it every single time before.

Has this approach worked? For now, absolutely. He certainly has picky days, but I wish I had a dollar for every time someone has said to me, 'I can't believe your son eats that.' Of course, it's still early days and when he turns four he may decide he wants to eat only pasta. But, at this point in time, I'm so grateful that each night I can have a relatively peaceful meal, where I serve my son the same dish that my husband and I are enjoying. From a nutrition perspective, I'm also grateful for the amazing health benefits that all those different ingredients give his growing body and mind.

Although I'm not a practising nutritionist, I do have nutrition qualifications and I'm well aware of the importance of a varied, healthy diet. Having said this, it's easy to make feeding children yet another facet of the ultra-competitive world of parenting where none of us feels like we measure up. So, while I believe in giving your baby nutritious homemade food when you can, it shouldn't interfere with the pleasure of being a mum or dad. If your happiness depends on a Friday night pizza and relaxing with a glass of red, I say cheers to that!

My hope is that this book will help guide you through those first few years of feeding your child. My philosophy is that feeding your baby should be fun, relaxed and not overly complicated or time consuming. I hope this book strengthens your confidence as a parent and helps you feel comfortable about serving your child the food that your family likes to eat. Above all, I hope it helps you to raise healthy children who can enjoy a home-cooked meal with you – surely one of life's simplest and greatest pleasures.

1

FEEDING
YOUR CHILD

WHY GOOD NUTRITION MATTERS

You've probably heard most of the usual advice. Give your child vegetables. Include fish in her diet. Don't give her too much salt. Give her plenty of fruit. Make sure she steers clear of trans fats. But what difference does all this actually make? Can it really affect your child's quality of life or how long she lives? The short answer is: absolutely.

You have the potential to dramatically influence your child's growth, immunity, intellectual performance, coordination, behaviour and mood, as well as her short-term and long-term health, simply with the food you put on her plate. Study after study has shown this to be true. For example, we now know beyond any shadow of a doubt that eating plenty of fruit and vegetables reduces the risk of heart disease, stroke and many cancers later in life. We also know that children who get plenty of calcium and vitamin D have stronger adult bones and have a lower risk of osteoporosis in old age. We've seen that children who are breastfed are at less risk of obesity and chronic disease later in life. And there's evidence that children who have good iron levels perform better in intelligence tests and have better motor coordination than iron-deficient children. We also now know that having a diet rich in omega-3 fats plays a significant role in a child's brain development and cognitive ability. It would be easy to write an entire book on the impact of childhood nutrition on later physical and mental health.

Really, this shouldn't come as any surprise. As living creatures, we are a product of the food we eat. From the time your baby is conceived, every cell that makes up her growing body is derived from food. Initially, her structure is built from the food her mum eats, via the umbilical cord and then breastmilk, and from around six months it comes increasingly from the food on her plate. Food is literally the building blocks that make up her entire body.

Understandably, this can be a little daunting for you as a parent. But, all you really need to know is that if your child eats a varied diet comprising plenty of fresh foods from each of the major food groups, she's likely to be meeting her nutritional needs. Having said that, one nutrient that does need to be singled out for special attention is iron, because many young children do not get enough. Vitamin D can also be a concern. I've included more detailed information about these later in this chapter.

Every meal you have with your child is an opportunity to enhance her life, both through the pleasure of sharing home-cooked food and through all the goodness that meal will give her rapidly developing mind and body. The relationship between food and health gives you enormous influence over the adult that your baby will become. By filling her early years with nutritious food, you give her an extraordinary head start in terms of realising her full mental and physical potential and her best health.

A VARIED DIET

There is no question that eating an apple is good for you. However, eating an apple every day over the course of a lifetime will have far fewer health benefits than eating an apple one day, a plum the next, an orange the following day, then a banana, kiwifruit and papaya.

Why is this? No single food (with the exception of breast-milk in the first six months of your baby's life) can provide all the nutrients your child needs. Each food contains different nutrients in varying levels, as well as important non-nutrients, like disease-fighting phytochemicals. The more varied your child's diet, the more likely it is that she will be receiving all the components she needs for optimal growth and health.

A WORD ON TREATS

I passionately believe that sweetness is an integral part of a well-lived life and I can think of nothing more miserable than a world without chocolate cake, crème caramels and lemon delicious pudding. This means that desserts and cookies are definitely part of my son's diet, particularly at parties. But, I'm also aware that for every brownie he eats, that's probably one less piece of broccoli and steak he'll want at lunch or dinnertime. That doesn't matter one scrap on a day-to-day basis, but all those micro decisions you make for your child eventually add up to the sum total of his childhood diet. And knowing how that diet is one of the main factors dictating my son's health – both tomorrow and when he's an old man – I'd like it to be as good as it can.

Rest assured that one chocolate-chip cookie won't do any harm at all. To the contrary, I believe your child should savour every delicious crumb. But if that one cookie replaces an orange every second day, or those takeaway fries replace your home-cooked fish and vegetables a couple of times a week, then those decisions will eventually add up and be reflected in your child's health.

Variety helps your child's body to extract the maximum benefit from each meal she eats. This is because there are lots of complicated relationships between different food components, which affect how the nutrients are absorbed and retained. For example, vitamin C helps iron absorption, while vitamin D helps calcium absorption. Having a varied diet provides your child's body with the best chance of being able to make the most of these nutrient interactions.

Variety can also decrease your child's exposure to toxins. For example, there are some foods that are more likely to contain pesticide residues than others. Even vitamins and minerals can be toxic in large quantities. For instance, regularly eating large quantities of liver can, over time, lead to vitamin A toxicity. Variety helps to limit your child's exposure to any one potential toxin.

A varied diet is also crucial to minimising fussy eating. If you only ever serve your child corn and beans, I'm willing to bet she won't touch spinach the first time she sees it at a friend's house. She's also more likely to be the child in the playground who says 'Yuck! What's that green stuff in your sandwich?' to the kid next to her munching on an avocado roll. Familiarity is crucial when it comes to acceptance. If she's used to seeing all sorts of different things on her plate, then she's more likely to be an adventurous eater.

EATING BY COLOUR

One way to make sure your child is getting plenty of variety is to make sure she eats lots of different-coloured foods. The colour of a food gives a good insight into its nutrient and phytochemical content, such as the bright orange of beta-carotene-rich carrots.

Typically, the darker the colour, the higher the nutrient and phytochemical content, which is why beetroots (beets), berries and dark green vegetables are all such excellent foods. (And it's one reason never to leave behind the dark green flesh that's closest to the skin of an avocado – it contains more nutrients than the lighter flesh).

THE MAJOR FOOD GROUPS

Having a basic understanding of the major food groups is the first step in ensuring you eat a healthy, varied diet. These food groups are just as relevant for your baby or toddler as they are for you.

GRAINS AND CEREALS

This food group includes bread, rice, pasta, noodles, cereal, polenta, couscous, oats, quinoa and barley. They are an important source of energy, which active babies and toddlers need.

With adults and older children, it is recommended that most grains and cereals be in a wholegrain form, such as wholemeal (whole-wheat) multigrain bread, brown rice and bran cereals. While whole grains are also beneficial for babies and toddlers, too much fibre can be hard for them to digest and can interfere with their nutrient absorption. Large quantities of fibre can also be very filling and put them off eating other nutrient-rich foods. So, at first, go a bit easy on wholegrain foods, and then you can transition to more and more whole grains as your child gets older.

Once your baby is established on solids, he should have about one to two serves of grains/cereals each day. By the time he's a toddler, this can be increased to four serves a day. One slice of sandwich bread is considered to be one serve, as is half a cup of cooked rice, pasta, noodles, quinoa or porridge. Do not be concerned if your child is eating less than this – there is an enormous variation in the amounts of food that healthy children eat.

VEGETABLES AND LEGUMES

This food group includes all vegetables, as well as legumes such as chickpeas, lentils and red kidney beans. Nuts and seeds are typically included in this group too.

Vegetables and legumes are an excellent source of vitamins and minerals, and they also contain different phytochemicals – substances that we now know play an important role in fighting disease.

Once your baby is well established on solids, he should be having some vegetables every day. A small amount is all that he needs – about two or three tablespoons of cooked vegetables each day. Don't be concerned if he's eating less than this, as milk is still his main food. When he's a toddler, and his milk feeds start to reduce, you can gradually increase his servings to about half a cup of cooked vegetables or legumes two to three times a day.

Don't get too fixated on these amounts. If my two-year-old son eats some vegetables or legumes a couple of times a day (like hummus and avocado on his sandwich and roast pumpkin with his dinner), including something green (a side of peas), I'm happy. I also give him ground seeds and nut pastes, like peanut and almond butter.

FRUIT

Fruit is a really convenient and easy way to get plenty of nutrients into your child's diet. Most babies and toddlers are quite happy to snack on a few blueberries or some banana. Nutritionally speaking, fruit juice is not the same as fruit, and you shouldn't think of it as a substitute.

Before your baby's first birthday, aim for a couple of teaspoons of fruit each day. Once he's a toddler, aim for one small piece (like an apricot or kiwifruit) or half a larger piece (like an apple or orange) once or twice a day. Some days he'll eat much more than this and other days he'll eat less. So long as he's having some fruit most days, he'll likely be getting about the right amount.

'Grains and cereals are an important source of energy, which active babies and toddlers need.'

'Dairy foods are a great source of calcium and protein – both of which are crucial for little growing bodies.'

MEAT AND EGGS

Red meat, chicken, fish, shellfish and eggs are excellent sources of protein, which children need to support their growing bodies. Protein is a vital building block of muscle, bone, blood and skin, and it performs a whole host of other important functions. Legumes and dairy foods are also plentiful sources of protein.

Red meat, dark chicken meat and eggs are also great sources of iron, and oily fish contains plenty of omega-3 fats. Before your baby turns one, he only needs a small serve each day (half to one egg or about two tablespoons of cooked meat). When he reaches his toddler years, his daily serve can be increased to about a half-cup of cooked meat, 100 g (3½ oz) of fish or one to two eggs.

DAIRY

Until your baby turns one, breastmilk or formula should be his main form of sustenance, with the amount of other food he consumes gradually increasing from the time he starts solids. Between six and 12 months, he should have about 600 ml (20 fl oz) of breastmilk or formula each day, although some babies will need more. Don't give him too much solid food at the expense of milk – at this age, milk is his most important food. Your baby can have additional dairy food in other forms, such as a couple of teaspoons of yoghurt or a small grating of cheese each day.

After your child's first birthday, you can gradually reduce his milk to about 250 ml (8½ fl oz/1 cup) each day as you increase his other foods. He should also be having about 80 g (3 oz/⅓ cup) yoghurt (a great source of probiotics) or a slice of cheese each day. Reduce his milk further if he's having much more yoghurt and cheese than this.

FATS AND OILS

Although you might see fat as the enemy, don't apply that thinking to your child. Babies and toddlers need fat in their diet for their proper physical development and brain function. Ideally, you should include fats from a variety of natural sources such as olive oil, avocados, nuts and seeds, milk, yoghurt, cheese, meats, eggs, oily fish and coconut. These will come packaged with a whole heap of other nutrients and will be far better for your baby and toddler than the fat in processed foods. Manufactured foods often contain 'trans fats', which increase blood cholesterol and heighten the risk of heart disease. There is also evidence that they increase inflammation and insulin resistance.

The best fats for your child are monounsaturated fats (found in avocado, olive oil, nuts, peanut butter and sesame seeds), as well as omega fats. Some saturated fats are fine for young children when they come from a natural food source – like meat and dairy – but you can switch to reduced-fat dairy when your child turns two. At this age, you should also start cutting the excess fat off his lamb chop and minimising his saturated fat from other sources, like cream, butter and sausages.

How do food groups relate to babies?

- Once your baby is well established on solids, he should be eating some food from each of the major food groups every day – grains and cereals, vegetables and legumes, fruit, meat and eggs, and dairy.

- Make sure he's also getting some fat in his diet, for proper growth and development.

- Until he turns one, breastmilk or formula is your child's most important food source. From six to 12 months, he needs about 600 ml (20 fl oz) a day. After his first birthday, gradually reduce his milk intake in favour of other foods, although he'll still need at least 250 ml (8½ floz/1 cup) a day (more if he's not eating other dairy foods).

- Don't overload your baby on whole grains and other high-fibre foods. They're fantastic for him in moderation, and as he gets older you can increase his intake, but too much fibre can interfere with a baby's nutrient uptake.

KEY NUTRIENTS

My great-grandmother Isabel Fulton apparently used to boast that her family had the highest grocery bills and the lowest doctor's bills. Even she, 90 years ago, recognised how the food she fed her children affected their health. If she were alive today, she probably wouldn't have the highest grocery bills – buying fresh ingredients instead of processed food or takeaway meals is almost certainly a cost saving in today's world. But, just as in the 1920s, her family would still be benefiting no end from all the nutrients in her home cooking. Here's some information about some of those nutrients and the role they play in your child's body.

VITAMINS

Vitamin	What it does	Best sources
Vitamin A	Important for healthy eyesight, night vision and growth. One of the precursors to vitamin A is beta-carotene – an antioxidant that your child's body converts to vitamin A.	Liver and eggs. Beta-carotene is found in dark leafy greens (such as spinach), broccoli, and orange fruits and vegetables (such as apricots, carrots, sweet potato and pumpkin).
Vitamin B6	Plays an important role in metabolism, helps to make red blood cells and also influences immune function and cognitive performance.	Meat, fish, poultry, starchy vegetables (such as potatoes), legumes, some fruits, liver and soy products.
Vitamin B12	Involved in the making of new cells and helps to maintain nerve cells.	Exclusively in animal-derived foods (and some fortified foods) – meat, fish, poultry, milk, cheese and eggs.
Folate	Helps with the growth and maintenance of all cells. May defend against heart disease and cancer.	Leafy green vegetables, legumes, seeds and liver.
Vitamin C	As an antioxidant, vitamin C helps minimise damage to cells and helps fight disease and infection. It also helps the body to make collagen and to absorb iron.	Many fruits and vegetables including citrus fruits, guavas, papayas, kiwifruit, strawberries, mangoes, capsicums (peppers), tomatoes, brussels sprouts, cauliflower and broccoli.
Vitamin D	Plays a vital role in bone health – enhances calcium absorption and supports bone formation.	Sunlight (your child's body makes vitamin D following exposure to sunlight), oily fish, eggs and liver.
Vitamin E	As an antioxidant, vitamin E helps minimise damage to cells and helps fight disease and infection. Deficiency is rare, although it can occur in premature babies born before the transfer of vitamin E from their mum that occurs in the final weeks of pregnancy.	Polyunsaturated plant oils, leafy green vegetables, whole grains, wheatgerm, nuts, seeds, liver and eggs.

A WORD ON VITAMIN D

Vitamin D plays a crucial role in bone health and a deficiency can cause rickets, a disease characterised by bowed legs and other skeletal problems. The best source of vitamin D is sunlight, which your child's body uses to make its own vitamin D. Breastmilk also contains vitamin D, although the precise amount is highly variable. Low vitamin D levels are often seen in women who wear a veil or who are dark-skinned (their greater pigmentation means they need to spend longer in the sun, without sunscreen, to make the same amount of vitamin D as a paler woman).

There is concern that the breastmilk of a woman with low vitamin D may not support the needs of her exclusively breastfed baby. In Australia and New Zealand, where there is usually plenty of sunshine, supplementation is officially recommended only in higher risk cases, namely breastfed babies of veiled and dark-skinned women. People in southern regions where there is less sunlight need to ensure they get adequate exposure. In the UK and US, it is routinely recommended that breastfed babies be given a vitamin D supplement. Vitamin D is added to formula milk, so formula-fed babies usually aren't at risk.

Although it is not a good idea for babies to be exposed to a lot of sun because of the risks of skin cancer, a few minutes of early morning and late afternoon sunlight is generally acceptable and can protect against vitamin D deficiency.

MINERALS

Mineral	What it does	Best sources
Calcium	Plays a critical role in the formation of bones and teeth. Active bone growth occurs from birth to about 20 years of age and peak bone mass is achieved around 30. A calcium-rich diet in childhood is crucial for maximising peak bone mass and lowering the risk of osteoporosis in old age.	Dairy foods (milk, yoghurt, cheese), tinned fish (so long as the soft bones are eaten too), oysters, almonds, bok choy, sesame seeds and tofu.
Iodine	Integral to thyroid function, which regulates body temperature, metabolism, growth, and nerve and muscle function.	Iodised salt, seafood, dairy products and bread (with the exception of organic and salt-free bread, all commercial bread in Australia and New Zealand must be made using iodised salt).
Iron	Carries oxygen in the blood, which is used for energy metabolism and also plays an important role in immunity and brain function.	Liver, red meat, dark chicken meat (leg and thigh), tinned oysters, eggs, dried fruits, legumes and fortified breakfast cereals.
Zinc	Supports the immune system, vital to wound healing, and involved in taste perception. Also affects brain function and influences learning performance and behaviour.	Fresh oysters, shellfish, red meat, dark chicken meat (leg and thigh), milk and yoghurt.

A WORD ON IRON

It is worth making a special mention of iron because iron deficiency is one of the most common and most widespread nutritional disorders in the world, particularly in children.

Babies and toddlers need an enormous amount of iron. The Australian and New Zealand recommended dietary intake (RDI) for babies aged six to 12 months is 11 mg/day and for toddlers aged from one to three years it is 9 mg/day. Recommendations in the US are roughly equivalent, although they're lower in the UK. Compare this with the adult male RDI of 8 mg/day and you start to get a sense of how much it is.

What happens if your child doesn't get enough iron? For a start, iron deficiency can weaken her immune system and her resistance to infection. It can also interfere with her growth, energy levels and motor function. There is also evidence that iron deficiency can affect your child's appetite and so make her more prone to fussy eating.

In recent years, we've also learnt a lot more about the impact of inadequate iron on a child's intellectual performance. Importantly, iron is used to make the neurotransmitters (brain chemicals) that regulate your child's ability to pay attention. Being iron deficient will lower her motivation to persevere with mentally demanding tasks as well as impair her overall cognitive development. Her learning and memory will be affected, so she won't be reaching her full potential when it comes to learning new words and numbers, and a whole range of other mental hurdles. Although iron deficiency can be diagnosed with a simple blood test, a child's brain is sensitive to low iron levels before the blood effects appear.

Babies are born with iron stores that start to deplete at around six months. From this time, you need to introduce plenty of iron-rich foods including meat, eggs and liver to maintain appropriate iron levels. Nevertheless, reaching the RDI targets isn't an easy task. For example, 50 g of cooked steak contains about 1.5 mg of iron, while an egg contains about 2 mg. Liver is a stand-out food, with 50 g of cooked chicken liver containing about 5.5 mg of iron. For vegetarians, getting enough iron is particularly difficult because the non-haem form of iron found in plant foods isn't absorbed as well as the haem form that is found in meat. Eating foods rich in vitamin C at the same time does improve the absorption of non-haem iron.

Although I'm an advocate of getting nutrients through food instead of supplements, I do think it's challenging to meet the iron RDI through food alone. Babies who are eating iron-enriched cereals and drinking formula will be getting additional iron through these sources. However, if you have a toddler who isn't eating many iron-rich foods, you may consider using a supplement. Don't overdo it, though – it is possible to take toxic amounts of iron. The upper level intake for babies and toddlers is 20 mg/day (which includes iron from diet as well as from supplements) and having more than this puts your child at risk of iron overload.

Finally, you need to keep an eye on your toddler's consumption of milk and juice. Drinking too much milk is often linked with iron deficiency because it can interfere with a child's appetite for other, iron-rich foods. So, definitely crack down on big glasses of milk or juice before lunch and dinner.

WHAT ARE OMEGA-3 FATS?

Omega-3 fats are known as 'essential' fats because the human body can't make them and so it's essential that your child gets them in her diet. Omega-3 fats play a very important role in your child's brain development as well as her vision. Breastmilk is rich in omega-3 fats, which is one reason scientists believe breastfed babies often score higher on intelligence tests and eyesight tests in later childhood. Scientists have also observed a relationship between infant omega-3 intake and improved motor development. Having a diet rich in omega-3 fats also helps to prevent blood clots, lowers blood pressure and reduces the risk of heart disease and stroke later in life.

You can actually increase the amount of omega-3 in your breastmilk by having a diet rich in omega-3 yourself. If you're taking a breastfeeding-specific multivitamin, you'll probably notice omega-3 fats (DHA and EPA) listed in the active ingredients. Once your child stops breastfeeding, you can keep up her intake by feeding her oily fish (like salmon, tuna and sardines), eggs from chickens on an omega-3 diet, chia seeds and linseeds.

WHAT ARE ANTIOXIDANTS?

In a nutshell, antioxidants are substances that help the body prevent and fight disease. The key ones include vitamins C and E, beta-carotene and the mineral selenium, but there are many more, including plenty of the phytochemicals.

Antioxidants fight the 'free radicals' in your child's body, which are basically the bad guys that cause cell damage and, in turn, ageing and disease. By feeding your toddler antioxidant-rich foods (such as berries, pomegranates, tomatoes, prunes, broccoli, brussels sprouts and spinach) you are helping her to fight coughs, colds and other infections, to heal from any cuts and scratches, and to generally stay in optimal health.

WHAT ARE PHYTOCHEMICALS?

Phytochemicals are compounds found in plant-derived foods (like fruit, vegetables, grains and spices) that give food its taste, colour and aroma. An example is lycopene, which makes tomatoes red, and the flavonoids found in blueberries. As it turns out, these clever little compounds have some pretty extraordinary disease-fighting power, and scientists believe they perform a huge variety of roles including acting as antioxidants, reducing clot formation, reducing inflammation, improving memory and, most significantly, protecting against cancer and heart disease.

There are many different types of phytochemicals (broccoli alone is thought to have about 10,000) and each performs a different role. For example, the saponins found in alfalfa sprouts appear to prevent cancer cells from multiplying, while the lutein in spinach and kale seems to protect the eyes against macular degeneration.

The presence of phytochemicals is one reason it's better to eat a varied diet, including plenty of fresh plant foods, instead of relying on supplements for good health.

WHAT ARE PROBIOTICS?

You've probably heard that yoghurt contains 'friendly bacteria' or 'probiotics' that do good things for your child's tummy. To give you a fuller picture, those bacteria – such as *Lactobacillus acidophilus* and bifidobacterium – are living micro-organisms that enhance the bacterial colonies in the digestive system. They're particularly good following a course of antibiotics, which destroy much of the good bacteria. Although research into the health benefits of probiotics is still unfolding, it appears that these micro-organisms play a potent role in supporting your child's immune system and alleviating diarrhoea and constipation. So, try to regularly include some yoghurt in your child's diet, preferably an unsweetened brand, and she can benefit from the calcium, potassium and zinc that comes with each serve too.

'Buy fruit and vegetables that are as fresh as possible. To preserve their nutrients, don't store them for too long and don't overcook them.'

PRESERVING NUTRIENTS IN YOUR COOKING

Most people have heard that steaming is better than boiling for preserving the nutrients in vegetables. While that's true, it only tells part of the story. To understand the full picture, you need to know that different nutrients are sensitive to different things. Some are particularly sensitive to heat, others to oxygen, and so on. While microwave cooking with little or no water is better than boiling for preserving vitamin C, it's not so good for preserving the vitamin B12 found in animal products. Also, although the water-soluble vitamins do leach out into cooking liquid, that's less worrying when you plan to drink that cooking liquid, as you do when you have a soup or casserole. The heat will destroy some vitamins, but at least you won't tip any survivors down the sink.

Minerals are typically more resistant to cooking than vitamins. For instance, according to nutrient retention data published by the US Department of Agriculture, a baked potato retains 100 per cent of its iron and calcium, but loses 20 per cent of its vitamin C and 10 per cent of its folate. However, minerals also leach out into cooking liquid, which is another reason it's best to cook in liquid only if you intend to hang on to it.

Here are some tips for maximising the nutrients in your food:

- When cooking vegetables, go for steaming, stir-frying or microwaving (using as little water as possible), instead of boiling.
- Try to avoid cooking for long periods at high heats.
- Cut up fruit just before eating. If you've squeezed a fresh juice, drink it straight away.
- Don't overcook fruit and vegetables – cook until just tender but still crisp.
- Store most fruit and vegetables in the fridge, rather than on the benchtop (tomatoes are one exception – the cold interferes with their lovely flavour).
- Seeds and nuts should also be kept in the fridge to stop them from turning rancid.
- When cooking with linseeds and other seeds high in omega-3 fats, minimise their exposure to heat (for example, sprinkle over porridge just before eating).
- Buy produce as fresh as possible and eat soon after buying. Local, in-season produce will likely be fresher than food that has travelled long distances.
- Go for home-cooked over manufactured food.

NUTRIENTS AFFECTED BY COOKING

Easily destroyed by heat	vitamin B1 (thiamin), vitamin C, folate, vitamin B6, vitamin E, omega-3 fats
Easily destroyed by oxygen (losses occur when foods are cut up, processed and stored)	vitamin C, folate, vitamin E, omega-3 fats
Easily destroyed by light	vitamin B2 (riboflavin), omega-3 fats
Easily destroyed by microwave cooking	vitamin B12
Easily lost in cooking liquid	all the water-soluble vitamins: the B-group vitamins (including folate) and vitamin C

BREASTFEEDING

There have been some big leaps over the last decade or so in our knowledge about the benefits of breastfeeding. It is now completely uncontroversial to say that, from a health perspective, breastfeeding is best for your child. We also now know that the health benefits continue beyond six months.

Sometimes, because of health or other complications, a woman or baby can't breastfeed. Thankfully, for mums and babies who are in this position, formula milk is an excellent substitute and it contains many of the same nutrients found in breastmilk. However, for most women breastfeeding is a viable option, although it's sometimes hard work at first. My own breastfeeding experience was pretty torturous. I had the most extraordinary pain to start with – it made my labour seem like a walk in the park. I would burst into tears every feed from the excruciating needle-like sensation and it made my first month of being a mum really hard. But, thankfully, it started to ease at about six weeks and feeding my son eventually became a total pleasure.

Because it suited my lifestyle and because I'm intimately aware of the health advantages, I ended up choosing to breastfeed until 18 months. However, had it not been for the support I received in those early weeks (as well as the mountain of research I'd read on the benefits), I'm sure I would have stopped much sooner. I recognise some mums would regard 18 months as an exceedingly long time, and others would think that I should have continued for at least another six months. But, that's what worked for me. If you breastfeed until your baby's first birthday, then you don't need to use formula at all – your baby can go straight to regular cow's milk.

The following information is very supportive of breastfeeding because, on the whole, the scientific evidence is extremely strong. At the end of the day, however, no scientist knows your situation like you do.

When my first child was three months, I returned to part-time work as a lawyer. I wasn't ready to give up breastfeeding, so I took a breast pump to work so I could express in a private room, and then I stored my milk in the office fridge (which did get a few laughs). It was a bit of an inconvenience, but after reading about all the benefits, I wanted to breastfeed until my son was at least nine months. Sometimes my mum would even bring him into work so I could give him a quick feed at my desk.

At first I was quite hesitant about expressing and storing milk at work, but part of me was pleased that I was showing my firm that breastfeeding is a normal thing for working mums to do. I figured that if my boss wanted me to come back to work so soon, then he needed to know that pumps and bottles were part of the picture! I think if we all breastfed and expressed at work, it would help break down any remaining weirdness people might feel about it. I've actually had a few of our new mums at work thank me since and say that because I was so open about it, expressing milk is now a really accepted part of our office culture!

Emily, mum of Jonathon (3) and Alex (1).

BENEFITS OF BREASTFEEDING FOR BABIES

- From a nutrition perspective, breastmilk contains every nutrient your baby needs for optimum physical and mental development.
- It contains antibodies and immune cells that protect him from illness, reduce his risk of infection and support his developing immune system. These protections are particularly vital for newborns, but they continue to benefit your baby for as long as you breastfeed him.
- Breastmilk contains omega-3 and omega-6 fats that work wonders for your baby's vision and brain development. Although these are now added to some formulas, the scientific research suggests that this doesn't consistently produce the same visual and cognitive benefits as breastmilk.
- The nutrients in breastmilk are more easily absorbed by your baby's body than those found in formula milk.
- Babies who are breastfed are less prone to gastro-intestinal infections and respiratory illness.
- Some studies have shown that breastfeeding for at least six months also reduces the risk of acute lymphocytic leukaemia.
- Some studies suggest that breastfeeding reduces your baby's risk of Sudden Infant Death Syndrome.
- Breastfeeding is good for your baby's jaw development – sucking a breast is different from sucking a bottle. There is evidence that breastfeeding may reduce malocclusion (misaligned teeth and bite).
- Breastmilk is believed to provide some protection against asthma, eczema, food allergy and coeliac disease. This is one reason that allergy associations often recommend breastfeeding during the period that solid foods are first being introduced.
- Breastfed children have a lower incidence of overweight and obesity in later life. Studies show that the longer a child is breastfed (up until nine months, when results plateau), the lower his obesity risk. There is also evidence that breastfed children have a lower risk of heart disease and diabetes.
- Breastfeeding is associated with lower blood pressure up to adolescence.
- There is also evidence that breastfed children have lower blood cholesterol as adults.
- Breastmilk is easily digested and breastfed babies tend not to get constipated.
- Breastmilk is sterile and hygienic.
- Numerous studies have shown that breastfed babies receive higher scores on intelligence tests than children who are formula fed. This is more pronounced in pre-term babies.
- A breastfed baby is exposed to a whole world of different flavours through his mum's breastmilk, whereas formula milk tastes the same every bottle. There is evidence that this early exposure to different tastes makes breastfed babies more open to eating a varied range of flavours and less likely to be picky eaters.
- A breastfed baby regulates his own appetite – he decides when he's had enough to eat and you won't really know how much he's consumed. This sets the stage for a relaxed approach to eating, where exact quantities aren't monitored.

What is 'weaning'?

The word 'weaning' can be a bit confusing. It is sometimes used to describe the introduction of solid food and sometimes to describe the end of breastfeeding. Since breastfeeding can ideally continue until a baby is 12 to 24 months – or older, if you and your baby like – the introduction of solid foods should certainly not spell the end of milk feeds. For this reason, in this book I use the term 'introducing solids' or 'introducing solid foods' instead of 'weaning'.

BENEFITS OF BREASTFEEDING FOR MOTHERS

- Breastfeeding accelerates your recovery from the birth by helping your uterus return to its pre-pregnancy size and by putting a stop to post-birth bleeding more quickly.
- Breastmilk is free and more convenient than formula – there are no bottles to sterilise or warm up.
- Breastfeeding typically delays the return of your period, which means that it acts as a natural contraceptive (although not a failproof one, so if you really don't want to fall pregnant again, you should use a back-up contraception).
- There is evidence that it reduces your risk of cervical cancer and pre-menopausal breast cancer.
- There is also evidence that it reduces your risk of heart disease.
- Breastfeeding burns kilojoules (yes, for the first time ever you can lose weight just sitting on the couch!) so it helps you to lose some of that pregnancy weight.
- If you care about the environment (and it's hard not to when you've just produced a member of the next generation) breastmilk has none of the environmental costs that come with the manufacture and packaging of formula.

DIET FOR MOTHERS WHO ARE BREASTFEEDING

The main thing you need to watch as a breastfeeding mum is how much alcohol you're drinking. Alcohol does enter your breastmilk and can stick around for hours after drinking. As a guide, if a 59 kg woman drinks two standard drinks, the alcohol clears from her milk about 3.5 hours later. If she drinks four standard drinks, it takes almost 7 hours to clear. You need to be careful because alcohol has been shown to interfere with babies' behaviour and sleeping patterns and also to impede their psychomotor development. It can also diminish your milk supply.

As boring as it is, the safest option for a breastfeeding mum is not to drink at all, particularly in the first month of your baby's life. If you decide to drink after this age, aim for no more than one to two standard drinks a day, and go for mostly alcohol-free days. You should time your breastfeeds so that you feed just before drinking, when there's no alcohol in your system. You might also like to have some expressed milk handy for the following feed.

You also need to be mindful of your coffee and tea intake, because caffeine makes its way into your breastmilk. One or two cups a day is generally considered to be fine, but if you're a big coffee or tea drinker, you might consider cutting down. Instead, replace caffeinated drinks with water, which breastfeeding mums need plenty of.

When my daughter was born I thought I might try to breastfeed her until she turned one. She is now two and we are still going. My main motivation for continuing is that she always rejected milk from a bottle or cup and has never really liked other dairy foods, like yoghurt and cheese. Although I'm trying to get her to eat more dairy, until she does, I feel that breastmilk is still an important part of her diet.

One of the hardest things about breastfeeding a toddler is other people's reactions. I often get comments like 'I can't believe you're *still* breastfeeding that child!' from family, friends and even total strangers. I'm fed up with having to explain myself and I do wish everyone was less opinionated. I strongly believe it is a decision for each mother to make based on her own instincts and that no one else should interfere.

Michelle, mum of Amelia (2).

As for avoiding common allergens, like peanuts, there is no evidence that this has any benefit for allergy prevention and it is no longer recommended. However, if your baby is suspected of having a cow's milk protein or soy allergy, your doctor may suggest that you stop eating the culprit in question (see page 32).

Try to eat a varied, healthy diet while you're breastfeeding. As a general rule, the more nutritious your diet, the more nutritious your breastmilk will be. However, in the case of some nutrients, such as calcium and folate, your body will take from your own stores to make sure your milk quality is maintained. So, in this case, you will be the one who suffers from any deficiency.

OVERCOMING PROBLEMS

It is very common to come up against at least one hurdle during your time breastfeeding, whether it is terrible pain to start, attachment problems, nipple soreness, mastitis, an oversupply of milk, an undersupply of milk, your baby refusing one or both breasts . . . the list goes on.

Thankfully, there are some fantastic government and private support services to help you sort through those problems so that you don't have a completely miserable time of it. Don't hesitate to call on those services – that's what they're there for, and the staff are usually very keen to help you out. I also found talking to other mums who'd had similar experiences a real comfort.

If you're having trouble finding the support you need, you might like to contact your local hospital for advice. Alternatively, here are some other sources of support:

- La Leche League (International): www.llli.org
- Australian Breastfeeding Association (Australia): www.breastfeeding.asn.au
- Association of Breastfeeding Mothers (UK): www.abm.me.uk
- The Breastfeeding Network (UK): www.nationalbreastfeedinghelpline.org.uk

BREASTFEEDING IN PUBLIC

I find it appalling that in this day and age we still hear stories of women who are made to feel uncomfortable about breastfeeding in public. Thankfully, many countries around the world have passed legislation to protect your right to breastfeed in public places.

In Australia, New Zealand, the UK and most US states, there are laws giving women the right to breastfeed in any public location. So, if a café or restaurant owner tells you to cover up or take your breastfeeding baby elsewhere, you should feel very comfortable about standing your ground and informing them that they're breaking the law.

How long can I keep expressed breastmilk?

You can keep expressed breastmilk in a sterile container in the fridge for up to three days. It's best to store it at the back of the fridge where the temperature is coldest. Frozen breastmilk can be stored in a freezer for up to three months. Once you've thawed frozen milk, use it within 24 hours and don't refreeze it.

Don't be tempted to keep any half-finished bottles of milk – bacteria can pass from your baby's mouth through the bottle, so leftovers should be discarded.

FORMULA FEEDING

If you're not breastfeeding, you should give your baby formula milk until she's 12 months old. After her first birthday, you can switch to regular cow's milk. Or, if you prefer, you can use a toddler formula instead. These are typically fortified with various nutrients, including iron.

Formula is made to be as close as possible to breastmilk and it's the only suitable alternative to breastmilk. There is a mind-boggling choice of different brands and types. The most common are standard cow's milk formulas, but variations include:

- **Whey-dominant formulas** – usually recommended for children under six months. Whey and casein are two types of protein found in cow's milk. Whey is easier to digest than casein, which is why it's usually the protein of choice for younger babies.
- **Casein-dominant formulas** – often labelled as a 'stage two' or 'follow-on' formula, casein-dominant formulas are usually recommended for children over six months and typically have more added iron. If your child has plenty of iron-rich foods, there is no need to switch to this kind of formula, and staying with whey-dominant may be better for your baby's digestion.
- **Formulas with added long-chain polyunsaturated fatty acids** – commonly marketed under 'premium' or 'gold' labels, these formulas have added omega-3 (and sometimes omega-6) fatty acids, such as DHA and AA, which are found in breastmilk. The impact of such supplementation has been the subject of enormous research, with mixed results. Some studies have shown it provides formula-fed babies with the same cognitive and visual acuity outcomes seen in breastfed babies, but others have found no benefit.
- **Anti-regurgitation formulas** – these have added thickening agents to help the formula stay down in babies diagnosed with reflux. They should only be used on medical advice, as there may be more appropriate ways of managing your baby's reflux.
- **Lactose-free formulas** – these are suitable for babies with lactose intolerance and should only be used on medical advice. Sometimes a temporary period of lactose intolerance arises after a bout of gastroenteritis. However, primary lactose intolerance is uncommon in babies under one and you may like a second opinion if you're given this diagnosis.
- **Hydrolysed formulas** – the cow's milk protein in hydrolysed formulas is changed with the aim of preventing sensitisation or allergy. As with other specialised formulas, it should only be used on medical advice. If your baby is diagnosed with a cow's milk protein allergy, your doctor may prescribe an extensively hydrolysed formula.

Soy- and goat's-milk-based formulas are also available. However, there is no evidence that they offer any benefit from an allergy prevention perspective. Where an allergy has been identified, breastmilk or a hydrolysed formula is generally preferred. You're best to seek medical advice in this situation.

It is crucial that you prepare your baby's formula precisely according to the instructions on the packet. Make sure everyone in the family is doing it properly. Getting the measurements wrong will mean that your baby will be getting too much or not enough energy. The results could be disastrous and will almost certainly affect her growth.

It's best to get the water temperature correct and then add the milk powder. Using boiling water and topping up with cold will destroy more of the heat-sensitive vitamins than if the correct temperature is used from the outset.

YOUR CHILD'S TASTE PREFERENCES

Given how much time we spend buying and cooking food for our children, it is interesting that so few of us understand how our children's taste preferences develop. But a little insight into the world of your baby's taste preferences and how they change over time can spare you the agony of a fussy eater down the track.

Children are born with an innate preference for sweet tastes and an innate dislike for bitter tastes. At birth, children are indifferent towards salt tastes and it is believed that salt taste perception does not develop until about four months of age. Despite these innate and early preferences, children develop in vastly different ways according to their food environment.

As a parent, you have an extraordinary amount of control over your child's long-term taste preferences. Given the central role of diet in our risk of certain cancers, heart disease and a whole range of health conditions, this gives you enormous power over your child's lifelong health.

MUM'S PREGNANCY AND BREASTFEEDING DIET

Your child's taste journey begins well before his first mouthful of solid foods. Children first experience taste in the womb, via the amniotic fluid, and then as a newborn, via breastmilk. There have been studies showing that infants whose mothers drink carrot juice during their third trimester of pregnancy or while breastfeeding are more likely to enjoy the taste of carrots. Other research shows that breastfed babies are more accepting of fruit and vegetables than formula-fed babies if their mothers regularly ate these foods themselves. Mums can expose their babies to different flavours by eating a varied diet during pregnancy and breastfeeding.

FIRST TASTES

Your baby's first year provides a great opportunity to introduce him to a vast array of different foods. As your child gets older, encouraging him to try a new food can get more difficult, so use these younger months to expand your child's palate as much as possible. And don't be in any doubt that your baby's early tastes are really significant. A number of scientific studies have shown that children's first tastes can shape their taste preferences for years to come. In one, children who were fed sweetened water during their first three months of life showed a higher preference for sweetened water at two years old. In another, children who were given sour-tasting protein hydrolysate formulas in the first year were significantly more likely to prefer sour-flavoured apple juices at four to five years old. Although researchers have yet to test the theory extensively, it is believed that the first months of life may constitute a 'sensitive period' for shaping flavour preferences, with lifelong consequences.

KEEP UP THE VARIETY

Once your child is over 12 months old, there is still a lot you can do to keep his palate expanding, particularly before his second birthday when food 'neophobia' – a fear of new foods – often starts to really kick in. Most importantly, keep introducing new and different foods, even if he's not keen. Repeated exposure is one of the key steps in building acceptance of a food. It may take up to 10 to 15 tastes of a food before your child will accept it, so definitely don't give up after a few rejections. I have been shocked at the number of times my son began eating a piece of food that I was dead sure he wouldn't touch and that I put on his plate merely so he would get used to seeing it alongside the rest of his dinner.

FAMILIARITY

Your child's familiarity with a food is believed to be the number one factor dictating whether or not he will eat it. The best way to build familiarity is to give your child plenty of opportunities to taste, see and touch different foods – both raw and cooked, in a variety of different forms – from the time he starts solids. Don't just give him peach purée, let him see and touch the whole fruit, point out its fuzzy skin and its hard stone, let him watch you taking a bite. I have also found it useful to verbally 'label' my son's foods while he's eating (see page 83), and I try to include something green with every lunch and dinner so that green food is a very normal part of his world.

WATCH THE SUGAR

The innate preference for sweet tastes and dislike of bitter tastes that children are born with probably accounts for why so many parents struggle to get their children eating greens, which can be on the bitter side. However, your child's innate preferences change over time depending on his diet. Just think how many adults enjoy the bitter taste of coffee. It is tempting to add sweetness to your baby's foods to get him to eat them. However, studies have shown that doing this is likely to create an even stronger preference for sweet foods. Your child will eventually learn to like the flavour of savoury, even bitter, foods – but only if you give him the chance.

GOOD ROLE MODELS

Although children are born with certain innate preferences, most taste preferences are learned over time, and the family diet is one of the key factors dictating which preferences a child will develop. So, if you never buy or eat pumpkin, your child can hardly be expected to form a liking for it. Numerous studies have shown that parental modelling significantly impacts a child's willingness to eat a particular food. If you want your child

to eat green beans, make sure you eat them too! However, if you don't like a certain food, you also shouldn't let that stop you from giving it to your baby.

PARENTAL RULES

Sometimes our best efforts to create healthy taste preferences completely backfire. Have you ever met an adult who despises brussels sprouts? I'm willing to bet he was forced to eat them as a child. We know now that tactics such as 'you cannot leave the table until you finish your broccoli' are most likely to produce a child with a lifelong hatred of broccoli. Furthermore, strict restrictions on a child's sugar consumption have been shown to create a *higher* preference for sugary foods. Current research suggests that the best approach is prudent restriction, which involves establishing a home environment in which unhealthy food isn't freely available, but when it is available, it isn't overly restricted. This approach and other tactics for minimising food fussiness are discussed in chapter 6.

YOUR OWN TASTE PREFERENCES

On countless occasions, I have seen parents choose less healthy food options for their child based on their own eating preferences. For example, I know lots of mums who choose to give their babies sweetened yoghurt instead of unflavoured yoghurt because they say 'I would never eat plain yoghurt – it's too sour! I certainly wouldn't expect my baby to eat it.' Similarly, I've seen parents add salt to their baby's vegetables because they themselves wouldn't eat them any other way, or give their child juice instead of water because they don't like plain water.

It's absolutely crucial not to assume your baby's taste preferences are the same as yours. I'm actually not a big fan of unsweetened yoghurt, but my son absolutely adores it. He also loves sardines and anchovies (in small doses because I'm mindful of the salt) – tastes that many adults would turn their noses up at. Considerable research has been done into children's taste preferences and we now know that they live in a very different sensory world to adults in terms of the tastes and intensities they like. By giving your child the chance to develop a liking for healthy, unsweetened, varied foods – even if they're not your favourites – you're giving him the best possible opportunity to develop life-long healthy eating habits.

IS YOUR CHILD A 'SUPERTASTER'?

Some people are born with a heightened sense of taste, partly thanks to the fact that they have a heap more tastebuds than most individuals. Known as 'supertasters', these people make up about a quarter of the population.

While this may sound like some kind of magical power, it can actually be quite a nuisance. Because supertasters have a particularly heightened sense of bitterness, they are less likely to enjoy green leafy vegetables, such as brussels sprouts, cabbage and spinach, and certain fruits like grapefruit. They also tend to be more sensitive to chilli, very sweet food and very fatty food. For example, they can more easily detect the difference between skim and full-cream milk.

How do I establish food familiarity?

Establishing food familiarity needn't just happen at mealtimes. Try pointing out all the different fruits and vegetables when your child is sitting in the trolley at the supermarket, or when he's looking up at Grandma's fruit bowl. Storytime is another great opportunity. My son hesitated when I gave him a plum one day, but when I reminded him that the Very Hungry Caterpillar ate three of them, he happily changed his mind. Even though my singing is pretty dismal, I've also called on a few Wiggles songs to tempt him to eat different foods, and they work a treat. When I make up bedtime stories, I always make sure the main character eats a few different vegetables along the way.

Unfortunately for their parents, child supertasters tend to be fussier eaters and will be less inclined to eat their vegetables. If you suspect your child is a supertaster (there are tests available to find out), don't give up on green vegetables. A tolerance can still be learned with repeated exposure and the right environment. However, you may find he prefers sweeter vegetables, like baby peas.

A WORD ON ORGANIC FOODS

One of the main benefits of organic produce is that it is free from most of the chemical residues that are found on conventionally grown foods. With this in mind, I particularly try to buy organic for those ingredients that I won't be peeling the skin off, like strawberries, apples, capsicums (peppers) and spinach. This approach is not perfect – sometimes chemical residues can be found deeper than the outer skin – but it's certainly a good start. I also buy organic meats and eggs because the farmers tend to

care about the animal's welfare, and fewer synthetic chemicals are used in the production process.

There's no question that organic methods are kinder to the environment, and ideally, all our food would be grown this way. But, sometimes organic food is simply not available or affordable. As for nutrient value, the evidence that organic foods contain more nutrients is quite patchy, so this isn't a compelling factor for me.

FOOD ALLERGIES

Food allergy is estimated to affect between 3 and 6 per cent of children in developed countries. Unfortunately, it seems to be on the rise, although no-one knows for sure why this is.

For any parent, food allergy can be a terrifying prospect. We've all heard in the news about the tragic deaths of children who've had a reaction to the slightest exposure to peanuts. However, it is important to remember that the vast majority of allergic reactions are not fatal and allergies can generally be managed well.

It's also comforting to know that many children outgrow their allergy. In the case of cow's milk, about 85 per cent of allergic children become tolerant by age three, while roughly half of egg-allergic children are tolerant by age three. Although peanut and seafood allergy is more persistent, about a quarter of children resolve this by age five.

Symptoms of an allergic reaction are varied and can involve eczema, hives, rashes, an itchy mouth, a swollen tongue, diarrhoea, vomiting, stomach cramps, a runny nose, red itchy eyes, breathing difficulties, wheezing, coughing and/or sneezing. The most serious symptom is anaphylaxis, which involves the respiratory and/or cardiovascular system and can be fatal. Adrenaline is typically the first line of treatment for severe reactions, and parents of allergic children may be advised to carry an auto-injector (such as the EpiPen or Anapen).

The precise cause of food allergy is not known. It seems likely that both genetic and environmental factors are responsible. No 'food allergy gene' has been found, but children born into families where there is a history of allergic disease are at greater risk. Children can also develop a food allergy where there is no family history.

As for environmental factors, a range of possible risk factors have been proposed by scientists, including exposure to cigarette smoke, birth via caesarean section, high maternal age, a particularly clean living environment with less exposure to bacteria, delayed introduction of allergenic foods, and low vitamin D status. However, none of these is a proven contributor and further research is required before definite links can be shown.

WHAT CAN PARENTS DO?

There is nothing you can do to completely avoid the risk of food allergy and, if your child is diagnosed with a food allergy, there is no cure. Avoiding the particular allergen is the only way of preventing a reaction. However, based on the current evidence, there are some steps you can take that may minimise the risk:

- Don't smoke during pregnancy.
- Provide a smoke-free environment for your baby.
- Exclusively breastfeed your baby until she starts solid foods (that is, go for breastmilk over formula, if that's viable for you).
- Keep breastfeeding as you introduce solids – breastmilk may assist in developing your baby's tolerance to new foods.
- Don't delay introducing common allergens like eggs and peanut butter – it is possible this may increase your baby's allergic risk.

Contrary to what you may have heard, you don't need to avoid peanuts or other common allergens during pregnancy or breastfeeding. There is no evidence that this provides any protection against allergy. However, if a baby is suspected of having a cow's milk protein allergy, her breastfeeding mother may be advised by her doctor to avoid dairy foods.

If you are giving your baby formula, speak with your doctor about which is the best one for her. For babies at very high risk of allergy (due to family history), a hydrolysed formula may be recommended. Don't be tempted to use soy or goat's milk formulas unless a doctor advises you to do so – there is no evidence they reduce allergy risk.

INTRODUCING COMMON ALLERGENS

Although any food can trigger a reaction, over 90 per cent of food allergies are caused by the following:

- cow's milk
- egg
- fish
- peanuts
- sesame
- shellfish
- soy
- tree nuts (almonds, cashews, walnuts and other nuts)
- wheat

Until a few years ago, it was commonly advised that parents delay the introduction of these foods, sometimes until two or four years, to minimise the likelihood of an allergic reaction. However, now we know that the best approach is to introduce common allergens at the same time as other foods. This even applies to children with a family history of food allergy – although it is best to discuss this with your doctor.

The reason for this change is that it is now believed that introducing common allergens earlier (at around six months) may have a protective effect. A major Australian study has found that infants introduced to cooked egg at four to six months were significantly less likely to develop egg allergy than those who waited until 12 months. It has also been noticed that there are much lower rates of peanut allergy in Israel, where peanuts are typically introduced in infancy, than in the UK, where their introduction has (until now) been widely delayed in line with former government guidelines.

Other foods that sometimes prompt a reaction include tomatoes, citrus fruits, berries and pineapple, typically in their raw form. Referred to as 'oral allergy syndrome', some children experience itching and swelling of the lips, tongue and mouth after eating these foods, although any fruit, vegetable or nut can prompt this reaction.

ALLERGIC 'SENSITISATION'

Unfortunately, you cannot breathe a sigh of relief after your child has her first taste of peanut or egg without any reaction. This is because 'sensitisation' to a food is the first step in developing an allergy. What happens is that following your baby's first exposure, her body decides that the food is a threat and puts in place a defence system in case she eats it again. Then, on the second exposure, this defence system kicks into gear and the allergic reaction occurs. So, it may not be until the second taste that you see a reaction.

However, frequently a reaction does occur following the first taste. This is because the initial exposure might have occurred undetected through other means – possibly via the skin, breastmilk or even inhalation. Furthermore, allergies can arise at any age, even as an adult. For this reason, it is good to be aware of allergy symptoms and get your child checked by a doctor if you're concerned.

INTRODUCING NEW FOODS

Contrary to what you may have heard, you do not need to wait several days before introducing new foods to your baby. Once you start solids at around six months, you should feel relaxed about introducing a couple of new foods each and every day.

If your child does end up showing signs of a food allergy or intolerance, it might take longer to identify the cause than if you waited between new foods, but there is no evidence that this approach puts her at greater allergy risk. It may actually reduce her risk because it means a larger range of food can be introduced over a shorter period of time.

Symptoms of an allergic reaction often occur within 20 minutes to two hours after eating, although severe reactions can also happen almost immediately. On the other hand, food intolerances usually take longer to appear – typically several hours, sometimes even days, after a food is eaten.

You should always closely supervise your child while she's eating and following meals (particularly when you're introducing new foods and common allergens) to keep an eye out for any adverse reactions.

A WORD ON COW'S MILK PROTEIN ALLERGY

If you have an unsettled baby suffering from reflux, it is quite possible she has a cow's milk protein allergy, as it is one of the more common baby food allergies. Your doctor may refer you to a paediatric gastroenterologist to have this investigated.

Unfortunately, this allergy is sometimes misdiagnosed as lactose intolerance, an enzyme deficiency that interferes with lactose digestion. Lactose intolerance in newborns is relatively rare (although it can arise temporarily after a bout of gastroenteritis), and some specialists have voiced concern that it is too often incorrectly named as the culprit. The recommended treatment – to move the baby to a lactose-free cow's milk formula that is typically rich in protein – may only make matters worse for a baby suffering with a cow's milk protein allergy.

If a baby is suspected of having a cow's milk protein allergy, her breastfeeding mother may be advised by her doctor to avoid dairy foods. Soy products may also be off the menu, because often babies who are allergic to cow's milk are also allergic to soy. Formula-fed babies may be advised to move to an extensively hydrolysed formula. You should consult your doctor about what's best for your baby, if she's allergic.

VEGETARIAN AND VEGAN DIETS

It is possible to raise a healthy child on a vegetarian diet, but there is no question that it requires careful planning to avoid nutrient deficiencies. The main concerns are:

- **Iron** – although iron is present in many non-meat foods, the 'haem' form found in meat products is the most absorbable. Young children need an enormous amount of iron for optimum growth and health (see page 18), and it is not easy to achieve this on a vegetarian diet. Feeding your child iron-fortified foods will help, as will giving him vitamin C-rich foods to assist with the iron absorption. Although some plant-foods are rich in iron, they sometimes contain substances that inhibit iron absorption, like the phytates in legumes.

- **Zinc** – the best source of zinc is meat, and zinc from plant sources is not particularly well absorbed, making this another potentially problematic nutrient for vegetarians. Furthermore, soy (a common ingredient in vegetarian cooking) interferes with zinc absorption. However, dairy foods are a reasonable source of zinc. If you intend to raise your child on a pescetarian diet, oysters, crab and prawns (shrimp) are good sources.

- **Vitamin B12** – this vitamin is only found in animal-derived (and some fortified) foods, so it's another one vegetarians need to watch out for. So long as your child eats eggs and dairy products, he shouldn't risk deficiency. Although fermented soy products (like miso) include vitamin B12, it is in an inactive, unavailable form and so they aren't a good source.

- **Protein** – there are many plant-based sources of protein such as whole grains, legumes, seeds, nuts and vegetables. So long as children on a vegetarian diet eat a good variety of these foods, they can typically meet their daily protein requirements. For a child who eats eggs and dairy products, the task is much easier because these are excellent 'high-quality proteins' – meaning they contain all the essential amino acids that the human body requires.

- **Omega-3 fats** – because a child on a vegetarian diet will be missing out on oily fish, which is a rich source of omega-3 fats, you will need to include plant-based sources like linseeds and walnuts. Breastmilk includes omega-3 fats (in varying amounts according to the mother's diet) and is one reason that a vegetarian child should be breastfed for as long as possible, preferably two years (or longer). Omega-3 supplements for children are typically made from fish oils.

- **Vitamin D** – as long as your child is getting sufficient exposure to sunlight, vitamin D is unlikely to be a problem. It is also found in fatty fish and eggs, and in fortified milks and margarines. However, diet alone rarely provides sufficient amounts, which is why some time in the sun is really important.

Deficiency in any of these nutrients can have serious health consequences for your child, so it's a good idea to talk with a nutritionist or dietician to work out a feasible diet for him. If you can avoid deficiencies, you may actually be doing your child a favour in the long term. Vegetarians tend to have lower blood pressure and lower rates of heart disease, cancer and obesity than meat eaters.

If you raise your child on a vegan diet, the risk of nutrient deficiency is even greater. In addition to the concerns above, calcium deficiency can be a real problem, as a vegan diet precludes dairy foods. Children on a vegan diet should be breastfed for as long as possible. Where this is not possible, a soy-based formula should be used for the first two years, as these are typically fortified with essential nutrients. Supplements may also be necessary. Consult a nutritionist or dietician to plan a suitable diet for your child.

GETTING STARTED

WHY HOMEMADE BABY FOOD IS BETTER

Feeding your baby commercial baby food instead of making your own is seriously tempting. You can now buy so many beautifully packaged organic options with flavour combinations that, frankly, sound quite delicious. They come in those handy pouch packages and they usually have no artificial ingredients. How can your home cooking improve on that? Well, trust me, it can. Here's how:

- Homemade food is often more nutritious. To ensure the long shelf lives of those preservative-free packs, the food is typically heated to very high temperatures, which can destroy many of the heat-sensitive vitamins like vitamin B1, folate and vitamin C. Sometimes those nutrients are added back in, but often they're not.
- Home cooking usually tastes better. Given how formative your baby's early months are in establishing taste preferences, you're definitely better off giving her food that tastes like your regular family meals.
- Commercial baby foods typically have a consistent taste that doesn't reflect seasonal variations. But your fruit purées, chicken casseroles and vegetable blends will taste quite different every time you make them, depending on how you've tweaked the ingredients. Even if you regularly rotate the packet flavours you offer, you'll never get the variation that's in your home cooking. Again, this variation plays a really important part in developing your baby's taste preferences to accept a range of different flavours.
- Packet foods have a smoother, more consistent texture than most home cooking. Even the lumpier ones tend to be smoother than home-made mashes. Although your baby may prefer this, she needs that lumpier texture for her chewing and jaw development.

- By making your child's food, you're sending her the message that cooking food from scratch instead of buying it from a packet or restaurant is the best way to live. It is extraordinary the extent to which parents' cooking habits shape their children. All the best cooks I know learnt almost everything from their families, and my friends who can't cook invariably say their parents didn't know how.
- When you make your baby's food, you are the one who decides whether the ingredients are fresh enough. You choose whether to remove the wilted leaves from the spinach and whether to cut out those brown bits from the avocado. I personally just don't trust that all manufacturers will have the same high standards that I do when it comes to quality control.
- Home cooking tends to be cheaper and more environmentally friendly, with less packaging.
- Many family meals can be puréed or mashed and are suitable for your baby from the time she starts solids. In light of this, buying commercial baby food doesn't make much sense. You don't have to make her a special, separate meal – give her what you're eating.

Having said this, there are definitely times that packet foods have their place, such as when you're travelling. I'm the first to confess that I loved having one of those little pouches handy when I took my baby on an aeroplane. As with most things, moderation is the key.

GETTING READY TO START SOLIDS – WHAT YOU'LL NEED

You've no doubt already spent a fortune on your new baby and I'm sure you don't want to go out and buy yet another round of stuff that is one day going to end up in a dusty pile in your garage. So, here's a list of the essentials you'll need to start on your feeding journey, as well as the optional extras:

- **Baby spoons** – regular metal teaspoons aren't suitable because they're too hard in your baby's mouth. There is a wide range of soft baby feeding spoons available, with different shapes and sizes according to age. Of course, if you're planning on doing baby-led weaning (see page 47), then you won't need to bother with baby spoons – although you might like to buy a shorter-handled one so that your baby can learn to feed himself.
- **Highchair** – this is not essential at first and you can feed your baby on your lap if you'd prefer, but you will need one soon enough. You might find that a highchair doesn't provide enough support for your younger baby, in which case you might prefer a moulded seat, such as a 'Bumbo'.
- **Bibs** – bibs are not vital at first, but as your baby grows and feeding gets messier, you'll be grateful for the extra laundry they spare you from. I started with soft cotton bibs and then moved to a plastic moulded one.
- **Steamer** – steaming food is a great way of preserving many of the nutrients. Of course, there are other ways of cooking food and a steamer is not essential, but it will certainly make your life easier.
- **Blender or food processor** – unless you're doing baby-led weaning, you'll need something that can blend your baby's food to a purée. I use a hand-held stick blender for smaller quantities (and to put straight in the pot) and a food processor for larger quantities. A food processor is still a fabulous kitchen addition long after your baby's first year. I use mine for making pastry, pesto, soups, meat for dumplings and all sorts of other deliciousness.
- **Steamer + blender combined** – you can now buy special baby-food makers that are a steamer and blender in one machine. Some even include a bottle sterilising and food reheating function. One great feature of some of these machines is that the steaming water (which contains nutrients that have leached during cooking) gets added back to the blended food. I confess that, as a kitchen-equipment addict, I have one of these, but it definitely falls in the category of luxury optional extras. A Thermomix is a similar concept in that it cooks and blends food, but it has far more capabilities and you'll use it long after your baby is finished with purées.
- **Purée storage containers** – given your baby will only eat tiny portions of food each day, it's useful to make large batches of purées and freeze them for later. You can use regular ice-cube trays for this purpose, but they often use BPA-containing plastic (see page 39) and typically don't have lids, in which case, you can cover tightly with plastic wrap (cling film). I prefer to use special-purpose baby purée storage containers.
- **Plastic mat** – some people find it useful to pop a plastic mat or newspaper under baby's highchair, particularly when he starts self-feeding. I personally never bothered, but you might find this handy.

PREPARING AND STORING FOOD

Like me, you probably find the subject of hygienic food preparation and storage mind-numbingly boring, but unfortunately it's terribly important. Food-borne illnesses are a real problem and they can make your baby seriously sick. In Australia alone, it's estimated there are over 5 million cases (across all age groups) of food-borne illness annually – that's almost a quarter of the population affected each year. To make sure your baby doesn't pick up a case of food poisoning, you need to take great care when preparing and storing her food.

PREPARING FOOD

- Wash your hands thoroughly with soap and water before preparing any food.
- Keep your kitchen clean and use different chopping boards and knives for meats and fruits/vegetables.
- Take care when cooking meat, chicken and seafood, which are breeding grounds for bacteria. It is particularly important to thoroughly cook minced (ground) meat and sausages until there is no more pink. They have had more exposure to human hands and bacteria than steaks, which are only exposed on the outside.
- Don't let any raw meat or egg come into contact with cooked or ready-to-eat food. Raw chicken, in particular, is a carrier of salmonella bacteria.
- If you've got a cut on your hand, use a fresh bandage or wear a disposable glove when preparing food. Old bandages can contain lots of harmful micro-organisms.

STORING FOOD

- Once you've prepared a batch of purées, put it straight into the fridge or freezer. Purées will last for up to three days in the fridge and several months in the freezer.

It's a good idea to note the date on the container so you don't lose track.

- The 'temperature danger zone' in which maximum bacterial growth occurs is from 5°C to 60°C. To avoid these temperatures, keep hot food steaming hot and cold food in the fridge or freezer.
- You need to take particular care with storing meats, as well as cooked rice, both of which are common food poisoning culprits. Pop leftovers in an airtight container and store them in the fridge straight away – don't leave them to cool on the benchtop.
- Don't freeze foods more than once. The exception to this is when you're dealing with a frozen raw ingredient like frozen peas or berries, which you then cook. So, for example, it's fine to put frozen peas in a cooked beef casserole and then freeze the casserole.
- Don't keep half-finished foods or drinks. If your child doesn't eat all of her meal, throw the rest away.

REHEATING FOOD

- When using one of your frozen purées (or other frozen meals), it is best to thaw it overnight in the fridge and then reheat it until it's steaming hot all the way through. Of course, allow the purée to cool before serving so you don't burn your baby's mouth. If you're in a rush, you might like to stir through a little yoghurt to cool the purée quickly.
- Don't reheat food more than once.
- It's best not to reheat food in plastic containers as toxins in the plastic can leach into your child's food. Instead, use a porcelain dish or teacup.
- It's not necessary to sterilise your baby's spoons, bowls or containers. Washing them in very hot, soapy water or in a hot dishwasher is fine.

COOKING METHODS

Flicking through the average baby cookbook, you'd be forgiven for thinking that steaming is the only option for cooking your baby's foods. It is certainly handy because you can cook a few different ingredients at once and you preserve more of the nutrients than with boiling, but it is by no means the only choice.

You should feel very relaxed about using the methods that you use to cook your meals for cooking your baby's purées and finger foods. I love roasting because it produces a lovely intense caramel flavour, but frying, grilling (broiling), baking, barbecuing and microwaving are all fine. As an alternative to steaming, you can also put your ingredients in a covered saucepan with just a dash

of water. I like to cook whole baby zucchini (courgettes) this way. I pop them in a pan and add a few millimetres of water, and cook them until almost tender. Then I take the lid off, drain off any remaining water (or keep the pan on the heat until it evaporates), toss through some olive oil and cook it for a couple of minutes to brown a little.

The only thing you do need to watch out for when cooking for your baby, particularly if you're barbecuing, is any charred, blackened bits. These are thought to be carcinogenic (cancer-causing) if eaten regularly and so should ideally not be part of a young child's diet.

A WORD ON BPA

BPA – short for Bisphenol A – is a not-so-nice chemical used in some plastics and in the lining of some packaging (such as metal cans) to protect food from contamination and extend its shelf life. The jury's still out on just how bad BPA is. Some jurisdictions, such as Canada, the European Union and certain US states, have banned the use of BPA because of concerns that it might cause abnormal growth in babies, including reproductive problems, and may be linked to heart disease and diabetes.

However, a number of expert bodies and food safety authorities around the world (including Food Standards Australia New Zealand) say that such bans are not supported by the weight of the scientific evidence. They say that the amounts of BPA consumed by most people are well within internationally set safe levels and there is no cause for concern. Although this is heartening, I still prefer to choose BPA-free bottles, spoons and storage containers for my household.

HOW MUCH FOOD TO OFFER

When you're a new parent it's really confusing to know how much food your baby should be eating and it's hard to get a straight answer. The reason for this ambiguity is that, in your baby's first year, milk is his main form of sustenance. So long as he's eating a variety of solid foods with an increasingly varied texture, the exact quantities aren't crucially important. What's more, different babies will eat very different amounts, which is another reason not to get too fixated on how much your baby is having.

When you first introduce your baby to solid food, it's just about the taste at first, and he may not swallow any at all. As a guide, you should start with a half to two teaspoons of food after a milk feed. Young babies have quite a strong tongue-extrusion reflex, which prompts them to push food out of their mouths. This starts to fade at around four to six months, but in some babies it is still quite pronounced at six months or older.

Don't be stressed if it takes a few weeks for your baby to get the hang of swallowing. In a Swedish study, it was found that babies took an average of 28 days from their first taste of food to eat more than two teaspoons (10 ml) daily, with younger babies overall taking longer to adjust than older babies. Interestingly, adjustment times almost doubled for each younger age bracket – so babies six months or older took an average of 12 days, while babies aged four to six months took an average of 25 days, and

babies under four months took an average of 42 days. Don't feel in any rush – this whole eating caper is a major change for your baby!

Once your baby is about seven months and is managing at least one to two tablespoons or more, you can start to move him to two meals a day, then eventually three, plus a couple of snacks. As for how soon he moves from one to three meals, you will need to be guided by him because babies vary dramatically. As a guide, many babies eat two to three tablespoons of food three times a day by some time between seven and nine months.

Remember also that the amounts your baby eats will vary considerably from day to day. Some days you will think he is surviving on virtually nothing, and others – particularly when he's having a growth spurt – he will shock you at what a guzzler he is. That's why it's better to assess how much he's having over a week, rather than a day. The best way of all to know whether he's getting enough food is by regularly checking his growth. If he's continuing to grow well and staying roughly on the same growth chart percentile curve, then he's doing just fine.

Once your baby is well established on solids, you should be aiming for good variety from each of the major food groups every day. Appropriate serving sizes for each are set out on pages 12 to 15.

With my first baby, I really struggled to find the time to do much home cooking and I tended to resort to packaged baby foods more often than not. By the time my daughter came along I was better organised and I had more time off, so she never got food from a packet. Now that they're older, it's amazing how they're such different eaters – my son is much fussier whereas my daughter will eat anything. I can't help but think those early months must have shaped their habits.

Emma, mum of Charlie (7) and Amelia (5).

HOW DO I KNOW WHEN MY BABY'S HAD ENOUGH?

Your baby will usually make it quite clear when he's had enough to eat by refusing to open his mouth, turning his head away or spitting out his food. As a general rule, you should respect your baby's full signs rather than continually trying to slip in 'just one more spoonful'. Studies have shown that babies have an innate ability to regulate their own appetite, and encouraging them to finish everything on their plate can interfere with this. You definitely shouldn't continue if your baby is getting upset – this will make mealtimes stressful and could set him up for bigger eating problems down the track. You also shouldn't ever force the spoon into his closed mouth, as again, this will create negative associations with eating.

If your baby never seems to show full signs and is always happy to have more, you should feel comfortable about giving him larger servings as long as he's also still getting plenty of breastmilk or formula (at least 600 ml/20 fl oz a day). Remember that milk is his main food in his first year. You will also need to keep an eye on his growth, particularly if he starts jumping up the percentile curves on his growth chart. Speak to your doctor if you're concerned that he's gaining too much weight.

MILK OR FOOD FIRST?

When you first start your baby on solids, you should offer him a meal after his milk feed. The reason for this is you don't want to feed him when he's too hungry – he'll find the spoon frustrating and will be looking for his milk. Also, for the first couple of months, food is really about getting him used to new tastes and textures – it's not about filling up his tummy and you don't want any dramatic reductions in how much milk he's drinking (particularly if he's breastfeeding). You can really think of solid food as a 'top-up' feed in the first couple of months. If you find he has no appetite for his solid food and he's not willing to have a taste, you can offer him food halfway through a milk feed instead.

By the time he's about eight or nine months, you should switch things around and offer him milk after his meal. But, unless he's a great little eater, avoid giving him a meal if he's ravenously hungry or really tired – at these times, he'll probably just want his milk and it's unfair to expect him to eat well.

My first son ate like a sparrow when he was a baby, and he still does. I remember being worried as I watched other parents feeding their children whole containers of purées, while Vincent would only have a few teaspoons. When my second son came along, he couldn't have been more different. He is a bit bigger physically and just loved his food from the word go. I could hardly keep up with how much he could eat – he always seemed to want more. Having been through this, I'm very aware that there's no 'one size fits all' when it comes to quantities. I think the best thing you can do is stay relaxed and just follow your child's lead.

Lucy, mum of Vincent (4), Chico (2) and Zoe (6 months).

FOODS AND DRINKS TO AVOID

Food/drink to avoid	Until which age?	Reason
Honey	12 months	Small risk of infant botulism.
Cow's milk as a drink	12 months	Can be a major contributor to iron deficiency anaemia because it is a poor source of iron and displaces meals and other milk drinks. Small amounts used in cooking are fine.
Goat's milk	12 months	High electrolyte and protein concentrations put a major strain on babies' developing kidneys. Low levels of vitamin B12 and folate create risk of deficiencies. Can also be a major contributor to iron deficiency anaemia.
Foods high in added sugar	12 months (preferably as long as possible)	Displace nutrient-dense foods, create a risk of dental damage and can create a stronger taste preference for sweet foods.
Sweet drinks (including juice and soft drinks)	12 months (preferably as long as possible)	Displace nutrient-dense foods and milk, and create a risk of dental damage.
Foods high in salt/sodium (e.g. processed foods, including bread)	12 months (preferably as long as possible)	Place too much strain on babies' developing kidneys. Can create a strong taste preference for salty foods, which can have longer-term health implications.
Raw or undercooked eggs Raw-egg products (e.g. homemade mayonnaise)	2 years	Risk of salmonella poisoning. Cook eggs until the whites have completely set and the yolks have started to thicken.
Reduced-fat or 'skim' dairy foods	2 years	Dietary fat derived from full-fat milk, yoghurt and cheese is an important source of energy for a growing infant. It also promotes the absorption of fat-soluble vitamins.
Hard, small and round foods (e.g. whole nuts, whole grapes)	3–5 years	Risk of choking (see page 49).
Uncooked fermented meats (e.g. salami)	5 years	Higher risk of food-borne illness (food poisoning). 'Heat-treated' or 'cooked' products are safe – check the label.
Raw sprouts (e.g. alfalfa, radish, mung bean sprouts)	5 years	Higher risk of food-borne illness (food poisoning).
Artificial sweeteners	As long as possible	There is very little data about the safety or risk of artificial sweeteners when consumed by infants and toddlers.
Tea and coffee Caffeinated soft drinks	As long as possible	High caffeine content overstimulates a child's nervous system. Tannins in tea bind with iron and other minerals, reducing absorption and contributing to iron deficiency.

'You can make grapes safer for your baby to eat by cutting them in halves or quarters.'

WHAT YOUR BABY SHOULD BE DRINKING

· | · | · | · | · | · | · | · | · | · | · | · | · | · | · | · | · | · | · | · | · | · | · | · | · | · | · | · |

BEFORE STARTING SOLIDS

Until your baby starts solids at around six months, she doesn't need to drink anything except breastmilk or formula milk. She does not routinely need water or juice, even on hot days, and definitely no sugar water!

One potential exception to this rule is where your baby has diarrhoea and vomiting. Babies are very vulnerable to dehydration, so you should seek medical advice without delay if your baby has both of these symptoms. Usually mothers are advised to breastfeed babies throughout a diarrhoea and vomiting illness, but an electrolyte solution may be recommended by your doctor (don't be tempted to offer lemonade or juice). If your baby is formula-fed, your doctor may advise you to cut down on milk feeds and to give more clear fluids until the illness passes.

You may also need to give your baby a little water if she's truly constipated. Constipation is uncommon in breastfed babies, and there is a huge variation in how often healthy breastfed babies pass a bowel motion (even every 10 days or longer). Formula-fed babies should be more frequent than this (every day or two). If your formula-fed baby has hard, dry or pebble-like poo, this is a sign of constipation. Check with your doctor about resolving any constipation problems – she may recommend extra drinks of cooled, boiled water or even a little diluted prune juice.

AFTER STARTING SOLIDS

Once your baby start solids, you can start offering her water to stop her from getting constipated and to help her kidneys process the waste products that come from food. In the early weeks, when she's only eating very small

amounts of food and still drinking plenty of milk, water is less critical, so don't worry if she's not interested.

By the time she's eight or nine months, make sure you offer water with or after every meal, and occasionally throughout the day. Water is particularly important to help her kidneys process high-protein meals and she risks dehydration if she's not getting any. It's not necessary to monitor precisely how much water she's drinking. As long as she's drinking a little and you're offering it regularly, she's probably getting about the right amount.

Having plenty of fluids is particularly important when your baby has diarrhoea or vomiting. When she's sick she may go off her food altogether and want only her milk. That's fine – you should feel very relaxed about stopping solid foods for a couple of days if she has a tummy bug. Just reintroduce it in small amounts as soon as she's ready.

Sometimes babies develop temporary lactose intolerance following a bout of gastroenteritis – you'll get signs of this because your baby's diarrhoea will return when she's back on her full milk feeds. If your baby is formula-fed, speak with your doctor about using a lactose-free formula for a couple of weeks while she recovers. Breastfed babies will be fine to continue with their breastmilk.

You can use cooled, boiled water until your baby's first birthday, however, from six months onwards babies are able to have water from the tap – but only if it's of a high-quality drinking standard. Don't use mineral water, as it often contains salt and other minerals in quantities that your baby doesn't need. Bottled still water with no added flavours is generally fine, although take care as it may not contain fluoride, which is important for dental health.

JUICE – AN OCCASIONAL TREAT

You may be tempted to add juice to your baby's water bottle to encourage her to drink water. Boring as it may sound, there are a few reasons that this is a bad idea:

- **Children need to develop a liking for the taste of water.** I know so many adults who refuse to drink water and instead go for soft drinks, sugary juices, coffee and tea because they've never developed a taste for water. These choices are inevitably reflected in their yellow-stained teeth and growing waistlines. If there's one lifelong gift you can give your child before she grows up and leaves home, it's a liking for plain old water.

- **Sucking on a bottle of juice is terrible for your child's teeth.** Just ask your dentist – she will probably be able to tell you instantly upon looking into your child's mouth whether she's a regular juice drinker or not. Drinking a small amount of juice as a one-off is all right – it's the constant sucking on a juice-filled bottle or cup that is a real dental nightmare because your child's teeth are continuously sitting in a sweet, acidic bath that erodes her enamel and builds plaque.

- **Too much juice contributes to the big problem of toddler iron deficiency.** How can juice possibly affect iron levels? The problem is that children have very small tummies. Give them a glass of juice at 4 p.m. and suddenly they're not all that hungry for dinner. For every cup of juice your toddler drinks, that's probably one less serving of chicken, steak or scrambled eggs, all of which she desperately needs to maintain good stores of iron and other nutrients.

- **Juice is often the culprit behind toddler diarrhoea.** Small tummies have a hard time absorbing the high amounts of fructose in juice, as well as a substance called 'sorbitol', which is naturally prevalent in apple and pear juice.

The approach I like to take is to buy my son a small glass of juice as a treat if we're out at a café, but not to have any in the house. As a result, he loves his water and asks for it often. He's never known any different so I'm sure he doesn't feel like he's being deprived

If you do decide to make juice a regular part of your child's diet, make sure you heavily dilute it: three parts water to one part juice. And remember that juice is no substitute for a lovely piece of fresh fruit.

A WORD ON BOTTLES AND CUPS

Your baby may love her bottle, but the time will come when she will need to learn to use a cup. A perfect time to begin is when she starts drinking water at around six months. It's a good idea to start teaching her how to drink from a lidded cup with a spout and eventually how to use a straw. This will make it easier for her to drink sitting upright, without having to tilt her head right back.

You may decide to use the cup for her water during the day, and keep her bottle for her milk feeds (which is a lovely time for a snuggle). Lots of parents give up the bottle altogether around their baby's first birthday if not earlier, but some keep it for milk feeds for a few months longer. You'll just need to resist the temptation to put her in bed with her bottle of milk. If she sucks right up until she falls asleep, the milk will stay pooled around her mouth for much of the night, doing damage to her teeth. Also avoid putting juice in her bottle, as the continual sucking is a major cause of tooth decay.

EATING WITH THE FAMILY

There are huge benefits to be gained from including your baby in family mealtimes from the time he starts solids. For a start, he will be seeing food in its whole form, instead of just as a purée, and you can give him some of the food from your plate to have a squish and a little try. He will also start developing a taste for your home cooking, which will definitely help in the battle against fussy eating down the track.

Your baby will also be learning that meals are a time for the family to sit down together and chat about the day's news. Even though he's not a great conversationalist yet, his little sponge brain will be picking up on the social aspects of mealtimes. He'll also be seeing that there is certain etiquette that needs to be followed.

I always aim for a television-free dinner. Time with my family is the most precious thing in my life – why would I let television impose on it? There are also studies that show that children who eat while watching television are more likely to want junk food and less likely to eat fruit and vegetables – good reasons to switch it off.

Of course, in the early months, it is virtually impossible to time dinner so that it fits in with your baby, so you might leave it to weekends to include him at the table. As your baby gets older and his routines change, you might be able to bring dinnertime forward. However, at the end of the day, your sanity is more important than having your baby at the table. If a relaxed late dinner with your partner is the highlight of your day, don't change a thing!

As your baby gets older and into the teenage years, try to keep up the family meals. The impact of family meals on children has been the subject of extensive studies around the world and we now know that they're linked with children eating more nutritious foods, performing better academically, having better psychological wellbeing, and being less likely to have an eating disorder or take drugs. One US study found that 12 and 13 year olds who had infrequent family dinners were almost five times more likely to have smoked cigarettes and six times more likely to have used marijuana than their peers who had frequent family dinners. It also found they were twice as likely to perform poorly at school. What's more, there is good evidence that families who eat together have better cohesion and connectedness. Definitely a plus when you have a moody teenager!

My husband usually works pretty late and when my daughter was 18 months, I began to feel a bit sorry that she was rarely getting to eat with us. So, I started sitting down for an early dinner with her at 6 p.m. and, to my surprise, it worked really well. She loved having a 'big girl' meal at the properly set table with me, and then when my husband came home and she was asleep, I could relax and sit down with a glass of wine or a cuppa and have a catch-up with him while he had his dinner. She's now three, and we're still finding this routine works really well.

Kaitlin, mum of Abigail (3).

BABY LED OR SPOONFED?

● | ● | ● | ● | ● | ● | ● | ● | ● | ● | ● | ● | ● | ● | ● | ● | ● | ● | ● | ● | ● | ● | ● | ● | ● | ● | ● | ● | ● | ● | ● | ● | ● | ●

WHAT IS 'BABY-LED WEANING'?

'Baby-led weaning' is an infant feeding philosophy that rejects the idea that babies should be fed puréed food from a spoon. Instead, it suggests that babies should be given finger food and encouraged to feed themselves from the time of starting solids at six months. One important feature of baby-led weaning is that the baby decides how much she eats – her parents do not put food in her mouth or try to cajole her into having more.

There has been a lot of attention recently given to this feeding approach, particularly in the UK, but it isn't new and many families have done it for generations. In fact, my parents largely raised my sister and me in this way – they just didn't have a name for it back then! Supporters of baby-led weaning say that it is preferable to conventional spoonfeeding because it helps teach children to enjoy food and reduces the likelihood of fussy eating.

Baby-led weaning encourages a more relaxed approach to eating, where babies are involved in family mealtimes and parents do not get too stressed about the quantities their child is eating. This approach – where children are given a range of healthy foods and the freedom to choose what and how much they eat – has been proven to be the most effective for minimising fussiness. However, there is no reason that a similar approach can't be taken with a baby who is spoonfed. It's just a matter of offering plenty of variety and finger foods, being attuned to signs that your baby has eaten enough, and staying relaxed at mealtimes.

How does baby-led weaning work?

- Baby feeds herself – her parents do not feed her with a spoon or put any food in her mouth.
- Baby does not start on purées and then gradually move to more textured foods. Instead, she has foods that she can pick up in her hands from the time of starting solids (at six months).
- Baby sits down with the rest of the family at mealtimes and is offered the same foods, so long as that food is appropriate for her.
- Baby decides how much food she will eat – her parents do not try to encourage her to eat more than what she wants.

For more information, see www.babyledweaning.com

We started baby-led weaning when Jasper was six months. For each meal, we sat him with us at the table and gave him foods like avocado, banana, steamed carrot sticks, broccoli and beans, which he played with, sucked and started to chew. As he became more coordinated, we gave him toast soldiers to dip into lentil soup or bolognese sauce.

At first, his main sustenance continued to be breast-milk but he loved exploring the new shapes and tastes. We found the process really contributed to his development – he would sort the food into colours, he started taking an interest in different ingredients and he learnt to sit at the table with us. Once he caught on to the concept, he quickly mastered the process of eating and enjoying his food.

Because he has always eaten what we're eating, Jasper is really adventurous in his tastes and will eat any cuisine from Indian to Japanese, and any food including oysters, prawns (shrimp) and brussels sprouts. He also understands the social aspects of sitting down to eat dinner as a family – this makes him a great dining companion. We'll definitely use baby-led weaning with Oliver when he's ready.

Geraldine and James, parents of Jasper (2) and Oliver (5 months)

POTENTIAL CONCERNS

Baby-led weaning can be a bit nerve-racking for parents because of the concern that a baby may choke on her finger food. However, supporters of baby-led weaning say that while gagging is common (a retching movement where the baby moves food away from her airway), choking is not. Although there is no supporting scientific evidence, it is believed that as long as the baby is sitting upright and she is the one to put food in her mouth, she is probably at no greater risk of choking than an adult. Nevertheless, they advise that a baby should never be left alone with food.

Some parents may be concerned that their child is not getting enough solid food, and therefore not enough iron and other nutrients, using a baby-led approach. It is certainly true that your baby's iron stores start to dip at six months, and need replenishing through solid food, as milk alone will no longer supply sufficient amounts. The amount of food a child eats using a baby-led weaning approach is highly individual. Some babies are simply more adept at feeding themselves than others. If a baby is managing to eat plenty of iron-rich foods by herself, then there will be no cause for concern. However, many babies will need some help, which is why official government guidelines often recommend that parents start their babies on iron-rich spoon foods (such as meat purées and fortified cereals) from around six months.

One major practical drawback for many parents is that baby-led weaning is seriously messy. If you're the kind of parent who is happy to put a big plastic mat or newspaper on the floor and just deal with the mess, then that will be no big deal. For me, I confess that I just couldn't bear the extraordinary mess my son managed to create, three meals a day, every day. However, mess should definitely not deter you from finger foods completely, as they do play a key role in your baby's development and should be a regular part of her diet (see page 89).

Another potential drawback is that baby-led weaning advises that your child should not start solids until she can sit with little or no support. This helps to minimise the risk of choking. This was a problem in my house because my son couldn't sit until he was almost eight months. In fact, unusually, he was crawling before he could sit. If your baby is unable to sit, or is delayed developmentally in any respect that may interfere with her ability to get food into her mouth or to chew and swallow, baby-led weaning is probably not suitable for her. Instead, start with puréed foods and introduce finger foods when she's ready.

I started Immy on baby-led weaning when she was six months. She took to it straight away and by seven months was happily feeding herself a whole range of different foods like strawberries and steamed baby corn. I didn't worry about precisely how much she was managing to eat because she was still getting plenty of breastmilk between meals. Now that she's two she'll eat just about anything. I've no doubt that baby-led weaning has nurtured her love of food.

Abby, mum of Imogen (2) and Hector (3 months).

A HYBRID APPROACH

Baby-led weaning works well for some babies. I've seen a number of babies raised exclusively on finger foods who thrived under this approach and who are excellent eaters now that they're toddlers. However, for many babies, particularly those who can't sit well by six months or who aren't adept at getting food to their mouths, some spoonfeeding, at least for the first three months, is likely to be the best option. And of course, your own sanity may demand that you regularly give your baby a puréed meal from a spoon, particularly when you're visiting or travelling.

I believe a happy balance can be drawn between the baby-led and conventional spoonfeeding methods.

To start, your baby may only eat puréed foods, but also have a lovely play with foods in their whole form at the same time, squishing and sometimes tasting them at her leisure. As she develops, you may increase the finger foods you offer and eventually do away with purées altogether. You'll soon get a sense of how she likes eating. If she doesn't like being spoonfed, you should feel very comfortable about giving it up when you think she's ready. Similarly, if she seems overwhelmed by finger foods, you might continue with spoonfeeding for a while longer, but continue offering finger food at the same time. Ultimately, taking a flexible, relaxed approach that works for you and your baby will offer the best outcome.

A WORD ON CHOKING

Choking occurs when an object slips into a child's windpipe and becomes so tightly lodged that it partly or completely cuts off her breathing. Without oxygen, the child may suffer brain damage or die.

One really scary thing is that, if a choking child's breathing is totally cut off, she will be completely silent (the voice box is in the windpipe and doesn't work when no air can push through). This is why you should never let your child eat unsupervised. If she choked, you may not hear her and then walk in the room to find her unconscious or dead.

Almost any food can cause choking, so it is impossible to rule out the risk entirely. However, some foods are more likely to be culprits, including whole nuts, whole grapes, whole small tomatoes, raw carrots, raw apple, marshmallows, hard or sticky lollies, chewing gum, popcorn, peanut butter, hot dogs and large chunks of meat.

It is tempting to cut up all of your child's food into very small pieces to minimise the risk of choking, but doing this for too long will deprive her of the opportunity to develop her chewing skills. By the time she's eight or nine months, she should be learning the skill of taking an appropriate-sized bite from a piece of food. However, foods that present obvious choking risks – such as whole grapes – should definitely be cut up.

Other ways of minimising your child's risk include:

- always supervising your child while she eats
- ensuring your child sits upright when she eats
- not letting your child eat when she's walking or running around or overexcited
- knowing what to do in the event of choking (consult a first aid organisation if you're unsure).

3

FIRST FOODS
AROUND 6 MONTHS

THE BEST AGE TO START SOLIDS

The best age to start solids is a controversial subject and official advice has changed over the decades. However, we know more about baby health and nutrition than ever before, and based on the current scientific evidence, around six months is now widely recommended as the ideal age.

What exactly does 'around six months' mean? National guidelines do not typically provide a precise definition for this term. However, one exception to this is the Australian guidelines, which state that 'around six months' means between 22 and 26 weeks (which equates to five to six months).

The World Health Organization actually recommends exclusive breastfeeding (that is, no solid foods) for a full six months. This timing is important in developing countries, where access to healthy foods can be limited, sterile, nutritious breastmilk is often the safest feeding option. However, in many developed countries, where fresh healthy produce is usually widely available, this recommendation is relaxed, with official government advice typically stating that infants should start solid foods at 'around' six months instead.

STARTING TOO EARLY

There are good reasons to follow the recommendation to wait until around six months before introducing solid foods to your baby. Starting too early can cause problems because:

- Breastmilk is the ultimate baby food, providing the best possible nutrition for a baby (see page 23). If solids are introduced too early, a baby may miss out on that precious breastmilk and his mum's milk supply may drop.

- Babies have immature digestive systems that simply can't cope with solid foods in the early months. Older babies, like adults, produce pancreatic enzymes that help them to digest food. However, these are virtually absent until three months and inadequate until around six months.

- Young babies have a strong tongue-extrusion reflex that prompts them to push out any hard objects put into their mouths, such as a spoon. In young infants, this can make spoon-feeding difficult for parents, potentially creating a stressful, pressured feeding environment for everyone. This reflex starts to fade around four months, although the timing varies among babies.

- Exposure to potentially unsafe microorganisms in foods can place a baby at an increased risk of diarrhoea and other health problems.

- Babies are born with immature kidneys, which develop during their first year. Solid foods, particularly those that have a high protein content or added salt, put added pressure on a baby's kidneys (which is particularly problematic when a baby is ill or unable to drink enough fluids). As a baby gets older, his developing kidneys are better able to cope with the waste products derived from solid foods.

- Younger babies take longer to adjust to eating solid food. A Swedish study found that babies aged under four months took an average of 42 days to eat more than two teaspoons of solid food daily, while babies six months and older took an average of just 12 days – over three times faster than their younger peers.

STARTING TOO LATE

Introducing solid foods much later than six months is also problematic. Here's why:

- At around six months, it becomes increasingly difficult to meet a baby's nutrient requirements from milk alone. A baby's growth may be affected if solid foods are not introduced around this time.
- In particular, iron and zinc stores, which build up during pregnancy, become depleted at around six months, and need to be restored through iron-rich foods, such as meats and iron-fortified cereals. Having a milk-only diet beyond six months puts a baby at risk of iron and zinc deficiency.
- There is some evidence that delaying the introduction of solids may increase the risk of food allergy (see page 30). Further scientific research is currently being done to determine whether or not this is true.
- The optimal development of motor skills, like chewing, can be affected if solid foods are delayed for too long.

WHAT ABOUT PREMATURE BABIES?

The recommendation of starting solids at around six months applies to healthy, term babies. The timing may vary for premature babies. Of particular concern, preterm infants can be at greater risk of iron and zinc deficiencies because they won't have had those last few weeks or even months in the womb when stores of these important nutrients are built up. For this reason, they may need to start iron-rich foods (or supplements) sooner than if they had been born at term. You should definitely speak with your doctor about what's best for your premmie bub.

SIGNS OF READINESS

As babies near the five- or six-month mark, they may start to show some signs that they're ready for solid food, such as reaching out for objects and putting them in their mouth, gnawing on their toys or knuckles and making chewing movements. They may even try to reach food from your plate to put in their mouth. If you're seeing some of these signs, and your baby is around six months, you might decide it's time to start solids.

Often people wrongly assume that if their baby starts waking in the night when he previously slept through, that's a sign he's ready for solids. Babies go through regular growth spurts in the early months and there will be times that they need extra milk feeds at night. Unfortunately for sleep-deprived mums, there is no evidence that starting solids earlier creates a better sleeper. And, even if this was the case, there are important health reasons not to do it.

WHAT IF I'M DOING BABY-LED WEANING?

If you've decided to try the baby-led weaning approach (see page 47), you should not start giving your baby finger foods until he is six months and can sit up straight and hold up his head. If he isn't sitting unsupported by six months, try starting with spoon-fed purées and then transition to a finger food-based diet a little later.

Do I have to start with rice cereal?

Absolutely not. The reason rice cereal is such a popular choice with so many parents is that it's usually iron-enriched, it's a cinch to prepare, it doesn't have a strong taste, and it's easy to mix it with breastmilk or formula to get the right consistency. But, if you would prefer not to use it, that's fine.

'There is no need to delay giving your baby eggs when introducing solids. Although, as with other common allergens, do watch out for any reaction.'

WHEN TO INTRODUCE CERTAIN FOODS

If you've had a baby any time in the last five or so years, you've probably been completely confused and a fair bit frustrated at the total lack of consistency in the advice given about when to introduce certain foods.

I remember when I started my son on solids I read one book that said don't give red meat until seven months, egg yolk until eight months (making sure it's well cooked) and egg white until 10 months. The next book I read said runny egg yolk, liver and brains make an ideal first food but not to give any vegetable from the 'nightshade' family, such as potato, as a first food. The third book said potato was an excellent first food. A fourth said no animal protein until two years! Yet another said it's fine to dive into casseroles, roast dinners and salads from six months. I was ready to have my very own toddler tantrum!

Part of the reason for this confusion is that in recent years, allergy experts have been doing a lot of research into how the timing of introducing particular foods affects the likelihood of a reaction. They previously thought that delaying certain foods, sometimes until the toddler years, minimised the chances of a reaction. However, under this approach, worldwide allergy rates seem to have skyrocketed. So they went back to the drawing board and did more research and they now believe the reverse is probably true – that introducing common allergens earlier may actually protect against allergies.

This actually makes your life much easier. The old methods of introducing foods in a very particular order over a six-month period made starting solids a high-maintenance task and created a lot of anxious parents along the way. So, you can breathe a big sigh of relief and read on.

The very latest thinking is this:

- When you start your baby on solids at around six months (see page 52), you don't need to delay introducing any food. In fact, delaying common allergens, like egg, appears to increase the chances of your baby being allergic.
- With the important exception of the contraband items on page 42, you can give your baby any food you like from the beginning, preferably lots of iron-rich foods.
- You don't need to worry about introducing foods in any particular order. It really doesn't make a difference whether you give rice cereal first, sweet potato next and then avocado. Or apple, then beef then pear. The idea that you need to follow a strict order is nonsense.
- You don't need to wait three to five days between each food. Although this will help you identify the cause if your child has a reaction, the majority of children won't have a reaction and the waiting game is a nuisance. Giving new foods in quick succession does not increase your child's allergy risk.
- Monitor your baby closely when you introduce the following nine foods, which cause over 90 per cent of food allergies: cow's milk, egg, fish, shellfish, peanuts, sesame, soy, tree nuts (such as almonds, cashews and walnuts) and wheat. If your baby has an allergy to one of these, you'll probably know about it within a few hours of her eating it, possibly even a few minutes. She may not have any reaction until the second or subsequent taste.
- If you have a family history of allergies, you should have a chat with your doctor, who may have particular, individual advice for your baby.

THE FIRST WEEK

Hurrah! The day you've decided to start your baby on solids has arrived and you're all set, with Grandpa ready to take photos. Or perhaps the decision has been less formal and you've simply been giving your baby soft squishy foods to play with, and now he's starting to put some in his mouth. Either way, you have a lot of fun – and mess – ahead of you.

Here are some questions you might have in preparation for the first mouthful:

Where should he sit? If you've got a highchair with a baby insert that provides enough support, that's great – time to put it to use. Otherwise a moulded seat (like a 'Bumbo'), a reasonably upright bouncer, a pram or even a car seat will work just fine. Or, if you prefer, there's always your lap.

What time? The best time is after a nap and a milk feed, when your baby will be well rested and not too hungry. You might like to wait half an hour or an hour after the milk feed so that he's had a chance to digest some of it. It's best to start him on solids at lunchtime, rather than in the evening, so that you can keep an eye on him for any reactions.

Which food? This is less crucial a decision than most books would have you believe. Lots of people start with rice cereal, which is a good source of iron (because it's enriched). I also quite like the idea of avocado or a root vegetable purée, like sweet potato or pumpkin. You could use a fruit purée too, although you might like to get your baby accustomed to some savoury tastes first.

The world will not come to an end if you start with a mixed purée, like apple and carrot. This is commonly not advised on the basis that it's best to check your child's reaction to each single ingredient before going for a mix. Perhaps this isn't a bad idea for the first few days, but it's unnecessarily conservative to continue with that approach for any length of time.

Whichever food you choose, your priority should be to include plenty of iron-rich foods in his diet as soon as possible, particularly if he's breastfed.

What temperature? Your baby's mouth is far more sensitive to heat than yours, so he will not be able to handle food at the same temperature that you can. The ideal temperature for his food is body temperature (which you can test on your wrist, just as you're probably used to doing with his milk). If it's too cold, you may find he rejects it.

What consistency? Your baby's first foods shouldn't be too thick. Remember, he has only been drinking milk until now. Mix in some of his milk (expressed breastmilk or formula) so that the purée or cereal is semi-liquid, a similar consistency to runny custard. As he becomes more accustomed to it you can start to make it thicker. Also, avoid any big lumps in the early weeks – they're a bit much for a young baby to cope with.

Here we go! Once your baby is happily seated, put about half a teaspoon of your chosen food on a baby spoon and place it gently against his lips. When he opens his mouth, slide in the spoon, then carefully remove it, allowing his gums and lips to take off the food. More than likely, he will push out most of the purée with his tongue on to his chin. Gently wipe it, and have another try. If he won't open his mouth for the spoon, you could try putting a little of the food on your (very clean) finger instead, and let him suck it off.

He may not actually swallow any of his first meal, and may be quite disinterested in what you're offering. Don't be dismayed if this happens – it's very normal. It will take him quite a few meals to get a hang of this eating business. Don't persist for too long, as he will soon get bored and upset. It's best if you're the judge of what's an appropriate time, but I would go for 15–20 minutes as the maximum (and only if he's in a happy mood).

How much? If he does swallow his first mouthful and seems to want more, don't give him more than about one tablespoon, just to allow his body to adjust. Over the coming days, you can increase the quantity according to his hunger. But, depending on their age, it will take many babies at least a few weeks to eat one to two tablespoons.

MEAL PLANNING

Below is a meal planner, simply to give you an example of how your baby's first week of solids could look. Recipes for each of the purée options are on the following pages.

However, you should feel relaxed about devising your own system instead. In fact, in many ways, it's better if you do because you'll be more likely to be using seasonal ingredients that you like having in your kitchen.

You'll see that each day calls for a different purée. That may sound time intensive, but if you have them prepared in advance in batches in the freezer, it's easier than you think. Also, three of the days are make-on-the-spot meals (Days 1, 3 and 4), and you should only make the quantity that you think your baby will eat for that meal. If you're time poor, you can repeat the same meal a few times. The benefit of mixing things up is that your baby is being exposed to lots of different ingredients, tastes and nutrients.

The planner presumes your baby is still on five breastmilk or formula milk feeds a day. If this is not the case, just introduce the solid food meal after whichever milk feed he has around lunchtime.

FIRST WEEK OF SOLID FOOD – SAMPLE MEAL PLANNER

	Early morning	Mid-morning	Lunch	Late afternoon or evening	Bedtime
Day 1	Milk feed	Milk feed	Milk feed, followed by rice cereal (mixed with breastmilk or formula milk)	Milk feed	Milk feed
Day 2	Milk feed	Milk feed	Milk feed, followed by rice cereal with Sweet potato purée (page 63)	Milk feed	Milk feed
Day 3	Milk feed	Milk feed	Milk feed, followed by Avocado purée (page 71)	Milk feed	Milk feed
Day 4	Milk feed	Milk feed	Milk feed, followed by rice cereal with Papaya purée (page 72)	Milk feed	Milk feed
Day 5	Milk feed	Milk feed	Milk feed, followed by Roasted parsnip and pumpkin purée (page 64)	Milk feed	Milk feed
Day 6	Milk feed	Milk feed	Milk feed, followed by Carrot and pear (page 73)	Milk feed	Milk feed
Day 7	Milk feed	Milk feed	Milk feed, followed by Beef and three-vegetable purée (page 76)	Milk feed	Milk feed

YOUR BABY'S RESPONSE

Don't expect your baby to eat much the first few weeks of starting solids. It will take her some time to get a handle on what she needs to do and it's likely that more will end up on her than in her to start with. On the other hand, you may have a baby who just adores eating from the word go and always wants more. Another possibility is that your baby eats well at first, then later refuses to eat. Below are some ways to handle these different scenarios.

MY BABY REFUSES TO EAT …

If your baby refuses to open her mouth at every meal and you're not managing to feed her any solid food, there are a few steps you can work through.

Firstly, if your baby is under six months, it may be that she's just too young for solid food. In this case, the best thing to do is wait a couple of weeks and then try again. It's amazing how a fortnight or so can make the world of difference to a baby's interest in food. In fact, I had this experience with my son, who started solids at about 23 weeks. He just wasn't interested, so I took a break and tried him again at 26 weeks and he was a really different baby by then.

If you're confident your baby is ready for solids, try to make sure you're relaxed, because she may be picking up on any tension you might be displaying. It really is important to keep mealtimes as positive as possible. Next, you can try to encourage her by opening your own mouth and even eating some of her food yourself – babies are great mimics and she may be happy to follow your lead.

If you don't have any luck on this front, you could try using a little distraction. Giving her a toy or having someone else nearby to keep the mood fun might help her to relax into eating. The television is an obvious distraction and it works wonders in many cases. However, in light of evidence that children who watch television while eating tend to have a greater preference for unhealthy foods, I'd advise that you minimise television during mealtimes. Use it only if you're desperate, but avoid it as part of your child's everyday eating routine.

Another possibility is that your baby doesn't like the spoon in her mouth. Popping a little purée on your clean finger for her to suck off, or trying her on soft, age-appropriate finger foods (see page 89), or even changing spoons might solve the problem.

Remember that lots of babies take weeks to eat one or two tablespoons of food, so don't worry if she's eating like a sparrow at first. However, if the problem of food refusal persists, you should get your doctor's advice because not eating (or experiencing pain or discomfort when eating) can be a sign of a more serious medical problem.

Above all, never force your baby to eat – and never use the opportunity of an open mouth when she's crying or coughing to get another spoonful in. You could cause physical or psychological damage and you're almost certainly going to make the problem worse.

MY BABY ALWAYS WANTS MORE …

Some babies are big eaters from the beginning and if you have one of these you're probably baffled by other parents who complain that their child won't eat. The only real dilemma for you is making sure your baby is still getting plenty of milk, which should remain her main form of sustenance until her first birthday. If she's still drinking plenty of breastmilk (or at least 600 ml of formula milk) each day, you should feel comfortable about giving her larger servings of solid food, although if she's jumping up the percentile curves on the growth chart, it's probably time for a word with your doctor.

It's never appropriate to put a baby on a weight-loss diet, particularly when your baby is eating healthy, home-cooked foods, but your doctor may have some advice on her weight. See pages 12 to 15 for information on serving sizes. Lots of babies lose their extra baby fat once they start walking and being more active.

MY BABY ATE WELL AT FIRST BUT NOW SHE JUST WANTS MILK …

It is very normal for babies to have highly variable days – even weeks and months – when it comes to eating. So, your baby who ate with great gusto at first may now have done a complete turn-around and want only her milk. Frustrating as it can be (trust me, I know), try to stay relaxed. Sometimes it's a sign that your baby is feeling a little under the weather, in which case a mostly milk diet for a few days may be the very best thing for her.

Alternatively, as she gets older and more independent, it may be the spoon feeding rather than the food she's objecting to. Switching to a finger food diet (see page 89) may keep the peace.

Often older babies get bored sitting in their high chair for any length of time. If your baby will happily eat in her pram when there's plenty to look at, but is kicking up a fuss at home, this may well be the problem. Try to keep mealtimes short and sweet, and you may need to resort to a little distraction to get her through. Again, finger foods may be a big help here because they'll keep your baby well occupied.

There is also the possibility that she's developed a medical problem that causes her to experience pain or discomfort during or following her meals. If you suspect this, chat with your doctor.

A WORD ON GLUTEN

Gluten is the name given to the various proteins found in wheat (gliadin), rye (secalin), barley (hordein) and oats (avenin). These proteins don't cause a problem for most people, but in those with coeliac disease, the immune system reacts abnormally to gluten and causes damage to the digestive system.

Unfortunately, there is no universal agreement among allergy experts as to when is the absolute best age to introduce gluten to minimise the chances of a baby developing coeliac disease. However, several studies have shown that children who have

gluten for the first time before four months or after seven months appear to be at an increased risk.

You may have read that you shouldn't give gluten before your baby is six months. However, this age is not set in concrete, and there is no firm evidence that giving it in small amounts from 22 weeks (the age at which you may have decided to start your baby on solids – see page 52) creates a larger or smaller risk. As with most things, it's about moderation. So, if you want to give your baby an occasional mouthful of gluten-containing food a few weeks before she turns six months, that's fine.

PURÉES FOR THE EARLY WEEKS

The conventional wisdom of baby feeding has been to be very cautious in the early weeks and months, slowly adding one ingredient to your baby's 'repertoire' every few days. We know now this is unnecessary and that it only complicates your life. Furthermore, it delays your baby's exposure to a range of important foods, which could even heighten his allergy risk.

You can start with single-ingredient purées for the first few tastes, but move to blends as soon as you wish. Although this does make it trickier if you are trying to pin down the cause of an allergic reaction, most babies will never have a reaction. Also, there are nine foods that cause most reactions (see page 55), so if you've given your baby one of them, it's likely to be the cause.

In the early weeks, it's a good idea to keep your purées quite smooth and not too thick. Your baby has only had milk until now, and he needs some time to adjust to this new world of food. As the weeks progress, you should start to make them thicker and add more texture.

The following recipes include lots of single-ingredient purées, the main reason being that I think it's lovely to let your child experience the pure taste of a single food. As you give him one, you might show him the whole form of that food and tell him its name. When it's convenient – such as with a mango purée – you might also give him a little piece to squish in his hands and lick off his fingers.

Single-ingredient purées are also great to have handy in the freezer so you can mix them with other purées and rice cereal to make up your own lovely combinations. Don't get too stuck on single-ingredient fruit and vegetable purées, though – remember that your baby needs plenty of iron-rich foods from the time of starting solids, so start him on meats too.

WILL FRUIT PURÉES GIVE MY BABY A SWEET TOOTH?

Some parents are concerned that the sweetness of fruit purées will give their baby a preference for sweet foods and deter them from eating vegetables. We now know that children are actually born with an innate preference for sweet tastes, as well as an innate dislike for bitter tastes.

However, these innate preferences are modified by a child's taste experiences. For this reason, it is important to regularly give your child food without any added sweetness so that he develops a liking for savoury foods, and eventually accepts the bitterness of certain vegetables.

This doesn't mean that fruit purées are off the menu. As with most things, balance and moderation are key. Exposing your child to a range of fruits from a young age is a crucial step in helping him to develop an acceptance of the many different fruit tastes. If you find he's reluctant to eat his vegetables or meat without some sweeter fruit purée stirred through them, try removing the fruit over time and don't give him fruit before a course of vegetables – save it for afterwards.

'It's lovely to let your child experience the pure taste of a single food. You could show him the whole form of that food, tell him its name and give him a little piece to squish in his hands.'

Left to right: Carrot purée; Sweet potato purée;
Roasted parsnip and pumpkin purée (page 64)

FIRST VEGETABLES

Root vegetables – such as carrot, sweet potato, pumpkin and parsnip – are lovely first vegetables for your baby. They have a naturally sweet flavour, and are unlikely to cause intolerances or allergies. Potato is also fine to offer as an early food, but it can get quite sticky when put in a blender, so it's best to push it through a sieve or use a mouli to purée it. However, if it's cooked well and is very soft, you can get away with processing it for just a short time (with added liquid). You might also find that your baby likes potato best when it is mixed with a sweeter vegetable, such as carrot or sweet potato.

CARROT PURÉE

MAKES ABOUT 1 CUP

Babies need some fat in their diet for proper growth, which is why I add a little knob of butter or a small dash of quality olive oil to my steamed-vegetable purées. This fat also helps your baby absorb the beta-carotene in the carrot – an antioxidant that converts to vitamin A and supports your baby's growth and vision.

2 large carrots
10 g (½ oz) butter
1–2 tablespoons water or your baby's milk

Peel and dice the carrot. Steam until tender (about 15 minutes). Add the butter and water or milk, and blend to a smooth consistency.

Set aside one serving and freeze the remainder in individual portions for later use. You may need to add some more liquid to get the consistency just right before serving to your baby.

* Suitable for freezing

SWEET POTATO PURÉE

MAKES ABOUT 1½ CUPS

You can also bake the sweet potato in a 200°C (400°F) oven with its skin on for 20 minutes or until tender, then scoop out the flesh.

1 sweet potato
10 g (½ oz) butter
2–3 tablespoons water or your baby's milk

Peel and roughly dice the sweet potato. Steam until tender (about 12–15 minutes). Add the butter and water or milk, and blend to a smooth consistency.

Set aside one serving and freeze the remainder in individual portions for later use. You may need to add some more liquid to get the consistency just right before serving to your baby.

* Suitable for freezing

You can stir a little iron-enriched rice cereal through any vegetable purée to give your baby an iron boost.

ROASTED PARSNIP AND PUMPKIN PURÉE

MAKES ABOUT 1 ¼ CUPS

• | • | • | • | • | • | • | • | • | • | • | • | • | • | •

Roasting is a lovely way of cooking vegetables. it brings out their natural sweetness and gives some depth and complexity to your baby's taste experiences. Avoid any excessive black charring as this is not so good for your baby.

1 parsnip
200 g (7 oz) pumpkin
1 tablespoon olive oil
80–100 ml (3–3 ½ fl oz) water or your
   baby's milk

Preheat the oven to 200°C (400°F). Peel and dice the parsnip and pumpkin. Place in a baking dish and toss with the oil. Roast for 35 minutes or until tender. Add the water or milk and blend to a smooth consistency.

Set aside one serving and freeze the remainder in individual portions for later use. You may need to add some more liquid to get the consistency just right before serving to your baby.

* Suitable for freezing

Orange root vegetables, like carrot, sweet potato and pumpkin, are a rich source of beta-carotene. This vitamin A precursor and antioxidant plays an important role in your baby's growth and her developing vision.

SWEET POTATO AND BROCCOLI PURÉE

MAKES ABOUT 2 CUPS

• | • | • | • | • | • | • | • | • | • | • | • | • | • | •

A combination of a root vegetable and a green vegetable makes an ideal early food for your baby. You can replace the sweet potato with potato, pumpkin or carrot, and the broccoli with zucchini (courgettes), peas or spinach.

1 sweet potato
75 g (2 ½ oz/1 ¼ cups) broccoli florets
10 g (½ oz) butter
3–4 tablespoons water or your baby's milk

Peel and dice the sweet potato. Steam the sweet potato and broccoli florets until tender (about 12–15 minutes for the sweet potato and 8 minutes for the broccoli). Add the butter and water or milk and blend to a smooth consistency.

Set aside one serving and freeze the remainder in individual portions for later use. You may need to add some more liquid to get the consistency just right before serving to your baby.

* Suitable for freezing

'Don't feel that steaming is your only option when cooking for your baby. I adore roasting because it produces a lovely intense caramel flavour.'

FIRST FRUITS

Most babies take to fruit like ducks to water, as they love the natural sweetness. You should feel relaxed about offering any fruit purée to your baby – apple, pear, papaya, mango – use whatever is in season and locally available. Another excellent first food is avocado (which is technically a fruit despite often being regarded as a vegetable) – it's highly nutritious and a great source of healthy fats.

APPLE PURÉE

MAKES ABOUT 1 CUP

When using apples, choose a sweet red or pink variety. Green apples can be a bit tart for your baby's tastebuds.

3 red or pink apples
1–2 tablespoons water or your baby's milk

Peel, core and roughly dice the apples. Steam until tender (about 10 minutes). Add the water or milk and blend to a smooth consistency.

Set aside one serving and freeze the remainder in individual portions for later use. You may need to add some more liquid to get the consistency just right before serving to your baby.

* Suitable for freezing

STRAWBERRY AND APPLE PURÉE

MAKES ABOUT 1 CUP

There's something quite magical about the combination of apple and strawberry. For some reason, it's better than the sum total of its parts.

2 red or pink apples
6 strawberries

Peel, core and chop the apples. Hull the strawberries. Steam the apple and strawberries until tender (about 10 minutes for the apple and 1–2 minutes for the strawberries). Blend until smooth.

Set aside one serving and freeze the remainder in individual portions for later use. You may need to add some liquid (a little water or your baby's milk) to get the consistency just right before serving to your baby.

* Suitable for freezing

PEAR PURÉE

MAKES ABOUT 1 CUP

• | • | • | • | • | • | • | • | • | • | • | • | • | •

Pears are easily digested and make a lovely introduction to fruit.

2 pears
1–2 tablespoons water or your baby's milk

Peel, core and roughly dice the pears. Steam until tender (about 10 minutes, depending on ripeness). Add the water or milk and blend to a smooth consistency.

Set aside one serving and freeze the remainder in individual portions for later use. You may need to add some more liquid to get the consistency just right before serving to your baby.

* Suitable for freezing

PEACH PURÉE

MAKES ABOUT 1 CUP

• | • | • | • | • | • | • | • | • | • | • | • | • | •

Make the most of summer's peaches and nectarines by stocking the freezer with some stone fruit purées.

3 ripe peaches

Drop the peaches into a saucepan of boiling water for 2 minutes. Remove and briefly run under cool water. Using your fingers, peel off the skins, remove the stones and chop the flesh. Blend to a smooth consistency.

Set aside one serving and freeze the remainder in individual portions for later use. You may need to add some liquid (a little water or your baby's milk) to get the consistency just right before serving to your baby.

* Suitable for freezing

APPLE, BLUEBERRY AND CINNAMON PURÉE

MAKES ABOUT 1 CUP

• | • | • | • | • | • | • | • | • | • | • | • | • | •

Cinnamon adds a lovely new flavour dimension to a fresh fruit purée.

2 red or pink apples
80 g (3 oz/½ cup) blueberries
small pinch of ground cinnamon

Peel, core and roughly dice the apples. Steam the apple and blueberries until tender (about 10 minutes for the apple and 1 minute for the blueberries). Blend with the cinnamon until smooth.

Set aside one serving and freeze the remainder in individual portions for later use. You may need to add some liquid (a little water or your baby's milk) to get the consistency just right before serving to your baby.

* Suitable for freezing

Blueberries have one of the highest antioxidant contents of any fruit. Be sure to wash them well, as pesticide residues may be present on the skins.

NO-COOK FRUIT PURÉES

It's always useful to have a number of different frozen fruit purées on hand for stirring through baby porridge for breakfast or serving after a vegetable purée for lunch. However, some of the best purées – such as banana, avocado, papaya and mango – don't need any cooking, so you can just peel and prepare them as you need. Mango and other stone fruits can be quite fibrous, so they're best puréed with a blender or food processor, but the others you can just mash with a fork.

BANANA AND AVOCADO PURÉE

MAKES 1 BABY SERVING

This is a wonderfully nutritious meal that can be prepared in a moment. Avocado and banana aren't great for freezing because they go brown, so just make enough to use for one meal.

2 cm (¾ in) slice banana
1–2 tablespoons avocado

Using a fork, mash the banana and avocado together to a smooth paste (or you can use a small blender). If you like, you can add a little of your baby's milk for a thinner consistency.

> **Avocado purée:** Avocado is also lovely on its own as a stand-alone meal. Simply mash or blend a suitable quantity for your baby and stir through a little of his milk if needed.

MANGO PURÉE

MAKES ABOUT 1½ CUPS

Mangoes, like many other orange fruits and vegetables, are a great source of beta-carotene. They're best in the summer months when they are sweet and readily available.

2 mangoes

Cut each cheek off the mango, score in a crisscross pattern with a knife and turn out to expose the cubes of flesh. Remove the flesh from the cheeks and stone, taking care to cut off any skin. Blend to a smooth consistency.

Set aside one serving and freeze the remainder in individual portions for later use. You may need to add some liquid (a little water or your baby's milk) to get the consistency just right before serving to your baby.

* Suitable for freezing

PAPAYA PURÉE

MAKES 1 BABY SERVING

● ı ● ı ● ı ● ı ● ı ● ı ● ı ● ı ● ı ●

If papaya is a fruit that you've always turned your nose up at, it's time to give it another try. It may be an acquired taste, but it has such great health benefits that it's worth learning to like it. Although you can freeze it, it's so easy to prepare that you're best to eat it fresh to avoid any nutrient loss from the defrosting process and to enjoy it at its best.

1–2 tablespoons ripe papaya

Remove the seeds from the papaya and scoop the flesh into a small bowl. Mash with a fork until smooth.

* Suitable for freezing

> Papaya is a little sweeter than pawpaw and is a rich source of calcium, phosphorus, iron and vitamins A, C and E. It also contains papain, a digestive enzyme that helps with intestinal health.

RICEY MANGO PURÉE

MAKES 1 BABY SERVING

● ı ● ı ● ı ● ı ● ı ● ı ● ı ● ı ● ı ● ı ●

I believe it's important for babies to taste fruit and vegetables without any added cereal. However, stirring some iron-enriched cereal through a purée from time to time is a good way to include more iron in a meal and to thicken a runny purée.

1–2 tablespoons baby rice cereal
1 tablespoon mango purée (page 71)

Prepare the baby rice cereal according to the instructions on the packet. Stir through the mango purée and serve.

> Most commercial baby cereals are pre-cooked and then dehydrated, so they don't need to be cooked – you can simply add the specified amount of milk or water and they're ready to go. However, always check the packet as some brands do require cooking.

MIXING THINGS UP

Once your baby has had her first few tastes without any adverse reactions, you can start to be more adventurous with her meals. Try preparing meat, vegetable and fruit combinations, and introduce new foods regularly. Grains, such as rice, oats, millet and quinoa, can be used, as can full-fat unflavoured yoghurt.

AVOCADO AND SWEET POTATO

MAKES 1 BABY SERVING

With their smooth, creamy texture and excellent nutrient credentials (a source of vitamin C, folate, fibre and good fats), avocados are a perfect baby food. Mashing them with sweet potato will help increase your baby's absorption of the beta-carotene in the sweet potato.

1–2 tablespoons sweet potato purée (page 63)
1–2 tablespoons avocado

Using a fork, mash the sweet potato purée and avocado together to a smooth paste. If you like, you can add a little of your baby's milk for a thinner consistency.

CARROT AND PEAR

MAKES ABOUT 1¾ CUPS

Who says fruit and vegetables can't be mixed? A root vegetable combined with pear or apple makes a healthy, delicious meal for your baby.

2 carrots
2 pears
1–2 tablespoons water or your baby's milk

Peel and dice the carrots. Peel, core and dice the pears. Steam the carrot and pear until tender (about 15 minutes for the carrot and 5–10 minutes for the pear). Add the water or milk and blend to a smooth consistency.

Set aside one serving and freeze the remainder in individual portions for later use. You may need to add some more liquid to get the consistency just right before serving to your baby.

* Suitable for freezing

FIRST CHICKEN PURÉE

MAKES ABOUT 2½ CUPS

· | · | · | · | · | · | · | · | · | · | · | · | · | · | · | · | · | · | · | · | · | · | · | · | · | · | · | · | · | ·

It's a good idea to include dark chicken meat (thigh and leg) in your baby's diet. It contains about twice as much iron and zinc as the white meat.

15 g (½ oz) butter
1 chicken breast fillet, diced
1 chicken thigh fillet, diced
1 small sweet potato, peeled and diced
1 small zucchini (courgette), peeled and diced
1 pear, peeled, cored and diced

Melt the butter in a deep frying pan or saucepan, add the chicken and sauté for 3–4 minutes or until golden brown. Add the sweet potato and 185 ml (6 fl oz/¾ cup) water. Simmer, covered, for 10 minutes. Add the zucchini and pear and cook for a further 5–7 minutes or until the vegetables and pear are tender and the chicken is cooked through.

Blend the ingredients, including the cooking liquid, until smooth, adding more liquid if needed.

Set aside one serving and freeze the remainder in individual portions for later use. You may need to add a little water to get the consistency just right before serving to your baby.

* Suitable for freezing

Unless your baby is following a vegetarian diet, you should introduce meats along with other solids at around six months as his iron levels will start to dip at this age and will need restoring through his foods. Iron deficiency is one of the most common childhood nutritional problems. It can affect your baby's growth and development, as well as his general health, so you need to take care that he is getting plenty of iron-rich foods.

Iron is found in a wide range of non-meat sources (such as legumes and dried fruits), but the 'haem' form found in meats is most absorbable. Chicken is a great meat to start on because of its gentle flavour and texture, but you can start with red meat or fish if you prefer.

Left to right: First chicken purée; Beef and three-vegetable purée (page 76); Fish, potato and broccoli purée (page 77)

BEEF AND THREE-VEGETABLE PURÉE

MAKES ABOUT 1½ CUPS

If you don't have time to slow-cook the casserole beef, you can buy high-quality, preservative-free minced (ground) beef instead. Simply brown the beef, add the carrot, pumpkin and water and cook for about 20 minutes before adding the peas.

1 tablespoon olive oil
250 g (9 oz) casserole beef
1 small carrot, peeled and diced
150 g (5 oz/1 cup) diced pumpkin
50 g (2 oz/⅓ cup) frozen peas

Heat the oil in a deep frying pan or saucepan. Add the beef and brown, stirring, for about 5 minutes. Pour in 375 ml (12½ fl oz/1½ cups) water, cover and cook at a gentle simmer (or in a 150°C/300°F oven) for 1 hour.

Add the diced carrot and pumpkin to the pan, adding 3 tablespoons water if there is not much liquid left, and cook for a further 20 minutes. Add the peas and cook for a further 2–3 minutes or until the vegetables are tender.

Blend the ingredients, including the cooking liquid, until smooth, adding more water if needed.

Set aside one serving and freeze the remainder in individual portions for later use. You may need to add some liquid (a little water or your baby's milk) to get the consistency just right before serving to your baby.

* Suitable for freezing

It is crucial to include plenty of iron-rich foods in your baby's diet so that she's not vulnerable to iron deficiency. Contrary to advice you may have heard, you can serve your baby meat from the time she starts solids at around six months.

FISH, POTATO AND BROCCOLI PURÉE

MAKES ABOUT 2¼ CUPS

Fish is a wonderfully nutritious food for your baby and it's a good idea to help him develop a taste for it early on. It is one of the more common allergens, so watch out for any reactions.

1 potato, peeled and diced
150 g (5 oz/2½ cups) broccoli florets
150 g (5 oz) white fish fillet, skin and
  bones removed, diced

Place the potato and 250 ml (8½ fl oz/1 cup) water in a saucepan. Bring to a simmer, cover and cook for 10 minutes.

Add the broccoli to the pan and simmer, covered, for 5 minutes. Add the fish and simmer, covered, for a further 3-4 minutes or until the fish is cooked through and the vegetables are tender.

Blend the ingredients, including the cooking liquid, until smooth, adding more water if needed.

Set aside one serving and freeze the remainder in individual portions for later use. You may need to add some liquid (a little water or your baby's milk) to get the consistency just right before serving to your baby.

* Suitable for freezing

Fish is a fantastic food for your baby. It is a good source of protein and is typically high in vitamin B12 and iodine. Oily fish, such as sardines and salmon, are also great sources of omega-3 fatty acids, which are important for brain development and cardiovascular health. One downside of some species of fish is that they contain high levels of mercury. Species to watch out for are:

- orange roughy (also known as 'sea perch')

- catfish

- shark (also known as 'flake')

- billfish (also known as 'swordfish', 'broadbill' and 'marlin').

You should try to avoid giving your baby any of these high-mercury species, and certainly no more than once a fortnight.

'Buy stone fruits in summer when they are cheap and plentiful. Freezing a batch of purees means your baby can continue enjoying them as the weather starts to cool.'

PEACH YOGHURT

MAKES 1 BABY SERVING

· | · | · | · | · | · | · | · | · | · | · | ·

You can introduce yoghurt into your baby's diet from six months. Use plain yoghurt to avoid giving your baby the added sugar contained in many flavoured yoghurts. Instead, add fresh puréed fruit, like peach, to give it a natural sweetness.

1–2 tablespoons plain yoghurt
1–2 tablespoons peach purée (page 68)

Stir the yoghurt and peach purée together until well combined. If the mixture is cold, you may need to microwave it for a few seconds to bring it to the right temperature for your baby. Make sure you stir it well to get rid of any 'hot spots' from the microwave.

When buying yoghurt and other dairy products for your baby, choose full-fat varieties. Children need this fat for optimal growth and development. You should use full-fat products until your baby is at least two years old. Make the switch to reduced-fat sometime after her second birthday.

BANANA AND STRAWBERRY QUINOA

MAKES ABOUT 3 CUPS

· | · | · | · | · | · | · | · | · | · | · | ·

This makes a delicious, creamy breakfast porridge that you can keep serving into the toddler years and beyond. Whenever I make this for my son, I love having a bowl too. Quinoa is a gluten-free seed that is highly nutritious, making it an excellent early food for your baby.

100 g (3½ oz/½ cup) quinoa
1 banana, chopped
6 strawberries, hulled and halved
pinch of ground cinnamon (optional)

Place the quinoa and 500 ml (17 fl oz/2 cups) water in a saucepan. Simmer over low heat, stirring occasionally, for 15–20 minutes or until soft (there should still be some liquid remaining).

Add the banana, strawberries and cinnamon. Simmer, stirring, for a further 5 minutes or until the fruit is tender.

Blend until smooth. You may need to add some liquid (a little water or your baby's milk) to get the consistency just right before serving to your baby.

Set aside one serving and freeze the remainder in individual portions for later use.

* Suitable for freezing

4

MORE TASTES AND TEXTURES
6–9 MONTHS

YOUR BABY AT SIX MONTHS

At six months your baby may be just starting his food journey, or may have had his first tastes several weeks ago. If he is just starting, read through the information in chapters 2 and 3. Contrary to what you may have heard, it is not necessary to introduce single ingredients in a very precise order over a matter of weeks or months. This will not reduce your child's allergy risk and will just make life unnecessarily complex for you. However, do remember that it will take your baby a little while to adjust to solid foods, and his first weeks will be much more about having little tastes than eating any great volume of food.

Your priority for your six-month-old baby should be incorporating plenty of iron-rich food into his diet. So you can start him on enriched rice cereal, meat purées and legumes straight away. This is because babies' iron levels start to deplete at this age. Just be mindful when serving him high-protein meals that he's also well hydrated (see page 44).

When blending your baby's purées, start very smooth at first and make sure the consistency is quite runny. As he gets the knack of eating, you can gradually transition to thicker, lumpier textures.

There is no reason you can't give your six month old appropriate finger food, like a nice soft piece of avocado (make sure you know how to manage the risk of choking – see page 49). However, some parents like to wait until eight or nine months, when their baby has better hand coordination and mouth control. Whenever you think he's ready, having plenty of finger foods is an important part of helping your baby develop a good relationship with food, as he'll learn the look, taste and feel of various foods in their whole form.

DIVERSE PURÉES AND MASHES

As your baby's menu expands, you shouldn't be at all timid in preparing him purées. The combinations are virtually endless. You can prepare the recipes in this chapter, or use the table on pages 84 and 85 to help you create your own. If you'd prefer not to cook separate baby meals, chapter 7 includes a large selection of family meals that can be puréed for your baby from six months onwards. In many ways, introducing him to family foods as soon as possible is the best approach, as he'll start developing a taste for your cooking and the meals your family likes to eat. It's also a significant time saving for you.

Remember, the more tastes your baby is exposed to at this age, the more likely he is to be accepting of a range of different foods as he grows. Variety is the key, so try to keep meals interesting for him.

As he gets the hang of eating, start to move to lumpier purées and mashes. These are very important for chewing development. If he kicks up a big fuss, you can make the transition more gradual, but make sure you're also giving him plenty of finger food for his chewing practice (see page 89).

PREPARING FOODS FOR PURÉEING

You can use almost any combination of ingredients in a purée. The table on pages 84 to 85 will get you started. It is not an exhaustive list – there are many other ingredients you could try. Just be careful that you don't use anything on the list of foods and drinks to avoid on page 42. It's a good idea to mix vegetables (and sometimes fruits) with a protein – such as broccoli and pumpkin with beef; or green beans, sweet potato and apple with chickpeas – so that your baby is getting a balanced diet.

A WORD ON VERBAL LABELLING

A friend of mine who works as a nanny once told me a story I found fascinating. She was looking after a two-year-old boy and and a two-year-old girl from different families. One day she made some meatballs for their lunch, but neither of them would touch them. So she said to the little boy, who liked sausages, 'These are sausages. You love sausages!' He instantly started devouring the meatballs. Still, the little girl wouldn't eat them. So, knowing that she was accustomed to eating rissoles, my friend turned to her and said, 'These are rissoles. You love rissoles!' With that, the little girl happily ate them too.

This is a story that would resonate with many parents and it's a perfect example of how familiarity dictates whether or not a child will eat a particular food. With this in mind, ever since my son was a young baby, I have always verbally 'labelled' his food.

Whenever he eats, I tell him a few times throughout his meal what he is eating. If he is eating it in a non-whole form, such as apricot pureé, I try to show him the whole form of the food and say, 'This is an apricot. You're eating apricot'.

When he was about 18 months, this started to pay serious dividends. Regularly, I would put food in front of him that he might not have eaten for a few weeks and he would just stare at it, not wanting to touch it. I would say, 'Those are chickpeas. You love chickpeas, remember?' When he heard the word 'chickpeas', it was as if a light bulb of recognition had switched on and he would start eating.

The principle is quite simple – the more foods your child is familiar with, the more diverse his diet will be. And, as a parent, there is virtually no limit to how you can build that familiarity (see page 29).

It's also helpful to have some fruit-only purées on hand, because they're great in the morning mixed with baby porridge, or after lunch or dinner for a healthy dessert.

When making your purées, simply follow the instructions on the following pages to cook each ingredient and then blend together to the desired consistency, adding some water or some of your baby's milk as needed. Cooking times will vary – there is no substitute for using your eyes, fingers and tastebuds to work out when food is cooked. Also, you needn't feel limited to steaming vegetables and fruits. Any cooking method you like is fine (see page 39).

You might also like to incorporate one of the additional ingredients from the list on page 86 – for example, seeds and nuts make a really nutritious booster for your purées.

Just grind them up so they are quite fine and won't pose a choking hazard.

Make sure that you thoroughly wash any fruits and vegetables that aren't peeled, such as strawberries, blueberries, spinach and green beans, particularly if they're not organic, as they may contain chemical residues that can be harmful to young children.

Mixed purées are a great way of giving your child plenty of variety. But don't forget the pleasure of eating a single ingredient too – a perfectly ripe peach or some mashed avocado. This will go a long way towards helping your baby develop a taste for different foods.

PREPARING INGREDIENTS FOR PURÉEING

Vegetables

Beetroot (beet)	Peel, dice and steam for 20 minutes or until tender.
Broccoli	Cut into florets, dice stem and steam for 8 minutes or until tender.
Brussels sprouts	Trim ends, discard outer few leaves, and steam for 10 minutes or until tender.
Carrot	Trim ends, peel, dice and steam for 15 minutes or until tender.
Cauliflower	Trim stem, cut into florets and steam for 8 minutes or until tender.
Corn	Frozen kernels: steam for 3–4 minutes or until tender, or cover and microwave on high for 2 minutes, stirring once. Fresh cobs: remove husk and steam for 5–6 minutes or until tender.
Green beans	Trim ends and steam for 8 minutes or until tender.
Parsnip	Trim ends, peel, dice and steam for 15 minutes or until tender.
Peas	Frozen: steam for 3 minutes or until tender, or microwave, covered, on high for 2–3 minutes, stirring once. Fresh peas take a little longer than frozen peas, which are precooked.
Potato	Peel, dice and steam for 15–20 minutes or until tender.
Pumpkin	Peel, dice and steam for 12–15 minutes or until tender.
Silverbeet (Swiss chard)	Cut stems from leaves and chop both. Steam stems for 15 minutes and leaves for 7 minutes or until tender.
Spinach	Trim ends, chop and steam for 8 minutes or until tender.
Squash	Trim ends, dice and steam for 10 minutes or until tender.
Swede (rutabaga)	Peel, dice and steam for 15 minutes or until tender.
Sweet potato	Peel, dice and steam for 12–15 minutes or until tender. Alternatively, bake whole in a 200°C (400°F) oven for 20 minutes or until tender; halve lengthways and scoop out the flesh.
Zucchini (courgette)	Trim ends, dice and steam for 7 minutes or until tender.

Fruits

Apple	Peel, core, dice and steam for 10 minutes or until tender.
Apricot	Cut into quarters and steam for 2–3 minutes or until tender. Peel skin off.
Blueberries	Other than washing, no preparation is required.
Mango	Remove skin and seed and dice.
Nashi (Asian pear)	Peel, core, dice and steam for 10 minutes or until tender.
Nectarine	Cut into quarters and steam for 2–3 minutes or until tender. Peel skin off.

Fruits (continued)

Peach	Cut into quarters and steam for 2–3 minutes or until tender. Peel skin off.
Pear	Peel, core, dice and steam for 5–10 minutes (depending on ripeness) or until tender.
Raspberries	Other than washing, no preparation is required.
Strawberries	Remove hulls, cut in half and steam for 1–2 minutes to soften.

Legumes

Beans (e.g. cannellini beans, red kidney beans)	Tinned legumes: rinse well and drain.
Chickpeas	Dried legumes: cover with water and soak overnight. The next day, drain and put in a saucepan, cover with water and simmer until tender.
Lentils	

Meats

Beef	There are so many ways to cook meats. You can cook simply in a frying pan with a little olive oil on medium heat until cooked through. You can roast in the oven by placing in a baking dish drizzled with some olive oil and cook at 180°C (350°F) until cooked. You might also like to barbecue (avoid too much black charring as this is thought to be carcinogenic).
Chicken	
Fish	
Kangaroo	If you are using chicken breast, you can poach it by covering with cool water and bringing to the boil, then reducing the heat and simmering for 10–15 minutes or until cooked through. The dark chicken meat (thigh and leg) is richer in zinc and iron than the breast, so make sure you offer this regularly too.
Lamb	
Pork	

Grains

Couscous	Couscous is a wheat product that's quick and easy to make. Choose instant or quick cooking couscous, which cooks in about 5 minutes, and follow the instructions on the packet. It's an excellent way to add texture to a meat or vegetable purée.
Pasta	You can buy tiny pasta stars – including gluten-free varieties – from some supermarkets, which are good for adding texture to purées. Any small pasta shapes will do the trick, although you will need to blend them (once cooked) for younger babies. Alternatively, give your baby larger pasta shapes, such as fusilli, as finger food. Most family pasta meals can be puréed.
Quinoa	Quinoa is a highly nutritious, grain-like seed. Use one part quinoa to two parts water and simmer, covered, for 15 minutes or until the liquid is absorbed and the quinoa turns opaque. Quinoa can be puréed for a younger baby and stirred through a purée for an older baby.
Rice (brown or white)	Cook rice according to the instructions on the packet. Rice can be puréed along with the other ingredients for a younger baby and stirred through a purée for an older baby.
	Brown rice is more nutritious than white rice, and it's also higher in fibre. Fibre is important for digestive health, but too much of it can put a strain on your baby and limit his nutrient absorption. Variety is the key, so try using brown rice sometimes and white rice other times.

INGREDIENTS TO ADD TO YOUR BABY'S PURÉES

Once you've made your purée, you might like to add one of the ingredients below for a healthy and tasty twist:

- **Yoghurt** – choose a full-fat, unflavoured variety and one with the healthy bacteria *Lactobacillus acidophilus* and bifidobacterium. These bacteria work wonders for your baby's digestive health and are also believed to provide overall support to your baby's immune system. It's best to add the yoghurt fresh, rather than freezing it with the rest of the purée, because freezing does kill some of those lovely little bacteria.
- **Cheese** – you can start to introduce a little grated cheese into your baby's diet from six months. Cheddar is a popular choice. Until your baby is 12 months, avoid soft cheeses like brie, because they're more likely to be the cause of food-borne illness. Take care to grate hard cheeses so that they don't pose a choking hazard.
- **Tofu** – tofu is soybean curd, and it's a good source of protein and calcium. Soft tofu is excellent blended with a fruit or vegetable purée.
- **Herbs** – finely chopped herbs can turn an otherwise bland purée into a lovely, flavoursome meal. Chives and parsley are usually well accepted.
- **Nut butters and ground nuts** – the latest research suggests there is no reason to delay introducing nuts, unless you have a family history of allergies. Don't just limit your baby to traditional peanut butter. You can now buy all sorts of lovely nut butters, including almond, brazil nut, cashew and macadamia.
- **Tahini** – made from ground sesame seeds, tahini is a good source of calcium.
- **LSA** – the abbreviation for 'linseed, sunflower and almond', a sprinkle of ground-up LSA gives a great boost to any purée.
- **Chia seeds** – chia is a rich plant-based source of omega-3 fats, dietary fibre, protein and antioxidants.

There's no need to grind chia seeds – you can just stir a quarter-teaspoon through a serving.
- **Vanilla and spices** – adding some pure vanilla extract to fruit purées adds another flavour dimension, as do gentle spices like cinnamon and nutmeg.

DEALING WITH A BABY WHO HATES LUMPS

If you have a baby who loves smooth purées but rejects anything with lumps and bumps, try these tips:

- Babies tend to prefer an overall lumpy purée to a smooth one with the occasional big, unexpected lump. Try to get the texture consistent throughout.
- Your baby might be anti-lump if he's used to eating commercial foods, which tend to be much smoother than homemade foods. Mix some of your homemade food with the commercial food, and gradually increase the proportion of homemade over a week or two.
- Babies tend to fuss over lumps more if the purée is otherwise quite watery. Make your purées slightly thicker (adding a little rice cereal can help), so the lumps don't stand out so much.
- Even if your baby doesn't like lumps on his spoon, he might be fine with finger foods. Some babies prefer smoother purées but will happily chew on a rusk or a piece of chicken. If you have one of these babies, that's fine. He'll be getting plenty of chewing practice with the finger foods. Just keep offering sticks of food and try making your purées more textured over time. Alternatively, you might like to phase out purées and take a baby-led weaning approach (see page 47).
- An aversion to texture can be a sign of a medical issue, such as gastro-oesophageal reflux. If you're concerned, speak to your doctor, who may refer you to a paediatric gastroenterologist.
- Don't give up! Babies who will only eat smooth purées and don't venture to lumpier mashes or finger foods tend to be much fussier eaters.

'Seeds and nuts make a wonderful addition to your baby's purées. Ground to a paste, they're an excellent nutritional booster for his developing brain and body.'

THREE MEALS A DAY

· | · | · | · | · | · | · | · | · | · | · | · | · | · | · | · | · | · | · | · | · | · | · | · | · | · | · | · |

By the time your baby is eight months, she will probably be eating three meals a day. Below is a meal planner that shows how a week of meals for an eight-month-old baby might look. Breakfast can be as simple as mixing baby porridge with some fruit purée, and for lunch and dinner your baby can just have a mashed or finger food version of whatever you're eating.

You should feel very comfortable about devising your own system, and about repeating meals throughout the week, although the more variety, the better. The planner presumes your baby is still on four breastmilk or formula milk feeds a day. However, some babies will be having less than this. Also offer your baby water after meals, and the occasional sip at other times through the day.

SAMPLE MEAL PLANNER FOR AN EIGHT MONTH OLD

	Breakfast	Mid-morning	Lunch	Mid-afternoon	Dinner	Bedtime
Day 1	Milk feed Baby bircher muesli (page 92)	Milk feed	Red lentils and vegetables (page 98)	Milk feed	One-pot chicken (page 214)	Milk feed
Day 2	Milk feed Apple purée (page 67) and yoghurt, boiled egg with toast fingers	Milk feed	Lamb and prune couscous (page 97)	Milk feed	Roasted beetroot and sweet potato with yoghurt (page 98)	Milk feed
Day 3	Milk feed Papaya porridge (page 92)	Milk feed	Creamy chicken bolognese with pasta stars (page 97)	Milk feed	Minestrone (page 195)	Milk feed
Day 4	Milk feed Banana and strawberry quinoa (page 79)	Milk feed	Red lentils and vegetables (page 98)	Milk feed	Coconut fish with vegetables (page 94)	Milk feed
Day 5	Milk feed Baby bircher muesli (page 92)	Milk feed	Carrot, pumpkin and ginger (page 93)	Milk feed	Spaghetti bolognese (page 200)	Milk feed
Day 6	Milk feed Mango purée (page 71) with baby porridge	Milk feed	Chicken and broccoli in cheese sauce (page 94)	Milk feed	Ratatouille (page 204)	Milk feed
Day 7	Milk feed Vanilla fruit compote (page 91) with yoghurt, toast fingers with avocado	Milk feed	Egg and avocado (page 93)	Milk feed	Slow-cooked lamb shanks (page 219)	Milk feed

A WORLD OF FINGER FOODS

If your baby is able to sit upright with little or no support, there is no reason you can't start offering him finger foods from the time you introduce him to solids, and certainly by eight or nine months. Seeing, smelling, tasting and touching different foods in their whole form is fascinating for a child, undoubtedly more amazing than any toy you can give him.

Of course, don't expect him to start munching and swallowing finger foods from the start. To begin with, they're just a fantastic plaything, good for squishing and making a great mess. But as the weeks progress, you will notice your baby start to get a good handle on them, get them to his own mouth, have a little gummy chew and – finally – swallow.

It's best not to get fixated on how quickly he's meeting these milestones or exactly how much he's managing to eat. Any kind of interaction with finger foods, even if it's just squashing a strawberry in his hands and licking his fingers, is opening his eyes to the amazing world of food and providing him with a lovely sensory experience. Don't see it is as a waste if the strawberry isn't eaten – it has served a very important purpose nonetheless.

When choosing finger foods, go for larger shapes that your baby is able to grasp, and avoid any choking hazards, such as nuts and whole grapes (see page 49). Make sure that your baby is sitting upright, and never give him food if he's not closely supervised, such as when he's being pushed in his pram or riding in his car seat.

To begin, finger foods should be soft so that your baby is able to mouth them. One exception is rusks, which should be hard enough that your baby can't bite the pieces off and choke on them.

Good beginner finger foods include:
- sticks of ripe banana, peach (skin removed) and avocado
- soft cooked pieces of fruit, such as apple and pear
- homemade rusks (page 93) or good-quality commercial rusks
- soft cooked vegetable fingers, such as sweet potato and carrot
- roasted red capsicum (pepper), with the skin removed
- omelette strips
- soft cooked broccoli or cauliflower florets, which you can dip in a little melted butter
- pieces of soft fish
- grated or shaved cheese

Once your baby has mastered these (and for some babies this might not happen until 10 months or older), he can move on to:
- avocado spread on toast fingers
- soft cooked pasta shapes, like fusilli or penne
- strawberries and raspberries (these can be a bit tricky for a young baby to hold)
- sandwich squares
- fritters and fish cakes
- rolled risotto balls (see page 199)
- strips of steak and chicken
- frittata fingers (see page 114)
- well-cooked or canned legumes, such as chickpeas, cannellini beans and red kidney beans (if using canned legumes, choose a 'no added salt' variety) – if you like, you can give them a little squish first to minimise the choking risk
- strips of French toast (see page 107)
- cheese sticks

VANILLA FRUIT COMPOTE

MAKES ABOUT 1½ CUPS

· ı ·

Because you'll probably want to eat all of this delicious compote yourself, you might like to make a double quantity so your baby doesn't miss out. Before blending, put aside your serving to have with your breakfast porridge or with a dollop of yoghurt or cream for dessert.

1 large peach
2 apricots
80 ml (3 fl oz/⅓ cup) pure apple juice
　or water
1 vanilla pod, split lengthways or ½ teaspoon
　vanilla extract
4 strawberries, halved

Drop the peach into a saucepan of boiling water for 1 minute. Remove and briefly run under cool water. Using your fingers, peel off the skin, remove the stone and chop the flesh. Cut the apricots into quarters.

Place the peach and apricot in a saucepan with the apple juice. Scrape the vanilla seeds into the pan, then add the vanilla pod. Bring to the boil, then cover and simmer over low heat for 5 minutes. Add the strawberries and simmer for a further 2 minutes or until the fruit is tender.

Remove and discard the vanilla pod, then blend to the desired consistency. Set aside one serving and freeze the remainder in individual portions for later use.

* Suitable for freezing

PAPAYA PORRIDGE

MAKES 1 BABY SERVING

• • • • • • • • • • • • • • • • • •

You can now buy high-quality baby porridges. They are iron-enriched, and often combine different cereals, like oats and millet. The vitamin C from the papaya will increase your baby's absorption of the iron in the cereal.

1–2 tablespoons baby porridge
1–2 tablespoons Papaya purée (page 72) or
   well-mashed papaya

Prepare the baby porridge according to the instructions on the packet (most are pre-cooked and just require water or your baby's milk to be added). Stir through the papaya and serve.

BABY BIRCHER MUESLI

MAKES 1 BABY SERVING

• • • • • • • • • • • • • • • • • •

If you have any frozen fruit purées on hand, it takes just moments to prepare your baby a really delicious baby bircher muesli. Use an iron-enriched baby porridge, as the iron stores that babies inherit from their mums at birth start to deplete at six months.

1–2 tablespoons baby porridge
1–2 tablespoons Strawberry and apple purée
   (page 67)
1–2 tablespoons plain yoghurt
small pinch of ground cinnamon

Prepare the baby porridge according to the instructions on the packet (most are pre-cooked and just require water or your baby's milk to be added). Stir through the purée, yoghurt and cinnamon, and serve.

You can use oatmeal instead of a commercial baby porridge if you prefer. It will certainly be a cheaper option. Oatmeal is simply finely ground rolled oats (but check the packet to make sure because the term 'oatmeal' can refer to different things). However, be aware that it won't be enriched with iron and it will require a little cooking. Covering the oatmeal with boiling water for a minute will usually be sufficient to cook it. Just make sure it cools before serving it to your baby.

You can also make your own baby porridge by finely grinding rolled oats and rolled millet in the food processor. Unlike commercial baby porridge, it won't be enriched with iron and will require cooking.

EGG AND AVOCADO

MAKES 3–4 BABY SERVINGS

• | • | • | • | • | • | • | • | • | • | • | • | • | • | •

Because the egg white is finely diced, rather than puréed, this is a good recipe for introducing your baby to a little more texture. If you want a smoother texture, you can blend the egg and avocado.

1 egg
1 avocado

Boil the egg for about 8 minutes or until cooked through. Peel off the shell and separate the yolk from the white.

Mash together the yolk and avocado until smooth. Finely dice the egg white and stir through the avocado mixture.

HOMEMADE RUSKS

MAKES 3–4 BABY SERVINGS

• | • | • | • | • | • | • | • | • | • | • | • | • | • | •

You can sprinkle the rusks with a little grated cheese before baking.

2 thick slices wholemeal (whole-wheat) bread,
  crusts removed

Preheat the oven to 120°C (250°F). Cut each slice of bread into three strips. Place on a baking tray and bake, turning occasionally, for about 1 hour or until dry and crisp. Store in an airtight container for 4–5 days.

CARROT, PUMPKIN AND GINGER

MAKES ABOUT 1½ CUPS

• | • | • | • | • | • | • | • | • | • | • | • | • | • | •

Purées are a fantastic way to introduce your baby to many different and even sophisticated flavours. If you often use ginger in your own cooking, you can start getting your baby accustomed to the taste of it now. Just remember, a little goes a long way.

2 carrots, diced
300 g (10½ oz) pumpkin, diced
1 small ginger slice, peeled
1 teaspoon butter
2 tablespoons water or your baby's milk

Steam the carrot, pumpkin and ginger for 15 minutes or until the vegetables are tender. Add the butter and water or milk and blend to the desired consistency.

Set aside one serving and freeze the remainder in individual portions for later use.

* Suitable for freezing

CHICKEN AND BROCCOLI IN CHEESE SAUCE

MAKES ABOUT 1½ CUPS

If your baby is not a keen milk drinker, using milk-based sauces in her purées is a good way to make sure she's getting enough. You can use formula milk to make the sauce – it has more nutrients, including iron, than cow's milk.

1 skinless chicken thigh fillet, diced
60 g (2 oz/1 cup) broccoli florets, diced
½ quantity Cheesy béchamel sauce (page 121)
2 tablespoons chopped parsley or chives, optional

Steam the chicken and broccoli for 8–10 minutes or until cooked through. Stir through the béchamel sauce and parsley or chives, and blend to the desired consistency, adding a little water or your baby's milk if needed.

Set aside one serving and freeze the remainder in individual portions for later use.

* Suitable for freezing

COCONUT FISH WITH VEGETABLES

MAKES ABOUT 2 CUPS

Puréed fish and vegetables can be a little bland, but the coconut milk gives this recipe a lovely flavour and creaminess. You might even like to set some aside for yourself to have with a bowl of rice – and you can always add some of the rice to your baby's purée too.

10 g (½ oz) butter
1 small leek or onion, diced
1 carrot, diced
250 ml (8½ fl oz/1 cup) coconut milk
150 g (5 oz) white fish fillet, skin and bones removed, diced
80 g (3 oz/½ cup) frozen peas
25 g (1 oz/½ cup) baby spinach leaves

Heat the butter in a small saucepan over medium heat. Add the onion and carrot and cook for 2 minutes or until starting to soften. Pour in the coconut milk and 125 ml (4 fl oz/½ cup) water and cook for 10 minutes or until the carrot is tender.

Add the fish and cook for a further 5 minutes. Add the peas and spinach and cook for a further 3 minutes or until tender. Blend to the desired consistency, adding a little more liquid if needed.

Set aside one serving and freeze the remainder in individual portions for later use.

* Suitable for freezing

CREAMY CHICKEN BOLOGNESE WITH PASTA STARS

MAKES ABOUT 3 CUPS

• I • I • I • I • I • I • I • I • I • I • I •

Stirring pasta stars through a smooth sauce is a great way to introduce some lumpier textures.

1 tablespoon olive oil
1 carrot, diced
1 celery stalk, diced
2 skinless chicken thigh fillets, diced
1 small onion, diced
1 garlic clove, diced
400 g (14 oz) can no-added-salt peeled
    chopped tomatoes
50 g (2 oz) cream cheese, softened
1 tablespoon cooked pasta stars

Heat the oil in a deep frying pan over medium heat and sauté the carrot and celery for 3 minutes. Add the chicken, onion and garlic and sauté for a further 5 minutes. Stir in the tomatoes and 125 ml (4 fl oz/½ cup) water, cover and simmer, stirring occasionally, for 10–15 minutes or until the vegetables are tender.

Remove from the heat and blend until smooth. Return to the saucepan and stir in the cream cheese over low heat until mixed through.

Set aside one serving and stir through the pasta stars. Freeze the remainder in individual portions for later use, adding freshly cooked pasta stars just before serving.

* Suitable for freezing

LAMB AND PRUNE COUSCOUS

MAKES ABOUT 2½ CUPS

• I • I • I • I • I • I • I • I • I • I • I •

Take your baby on a tastebud trip to Morocco – this delicious purée is like a mini tagine.

You can make this with 400 g (14 oz) of diced casserole lamb instead of lamb fillet. Double the quantity of water and simmer very gently for 1 hour.

2 tablespoons olive oil
1 small onion, diced
1 garlic clove, diced
250 g (9 oz) diced lamb fillet
6 pitted prunes
½ teaspoon ground cinnamon
1 teaspoon chopped parsley, optional
3 tablespoons instant couscous

Heat the oil in a saucepan over medium heat. Cook the onion and garlic for about 5 minutes or until the onion is soft but not brown. Add the diced lamb and brown for 3–5 minutes. Add the prunes, cinnamon and 250 ml (8½ fl oz/1 cup) water, cover and simmer for 5–10 minutes.

Remove from the heat, add the parsley and blend until smooth. Return to the saucepan and gently reheat. Remove from the heat and stir in the couscous. Cover and set aside for 6 minutes.

Set aside one serving and freeze the remainder in individual portions for later use.

* Suitable for freezing

RED LENTILS AND VEGETABLES

MAKES ABOUT 2½ CUPS

• • • • • • • • • • • • • • • • • •

Lentils are a source of protein and iron, making them a great food for your baby. Unlike some other legumes, split red lentils cook quite quickly and don't require soaking.

1 tablespoon olive oil
1 small onion, diced
1 carrot, peeled and diced
1 small sweet potato, peeled and diced
3 tablespoons split red lentils
375 ml (12½ fl oz/1½ cups) Chicken stock (page 190) or water
small pinch of ground cumin, optional

Heat the oil in a saucepan over medium heat. Cook the onion and carrot for about 5 minutes or until the onion is soft.

Add the sweet potato, red lentils, stock and cumin. Bring to the boil, then reduce the heat, cover and simmer for 20 minutes or until the lentils and vegetables are tender. Blend to the desired consistency, adding a little more liquid if needed.

Set aside one serving and freeze the remainder in individual portions for later use.

* Suitable for freezing

ROASTED BEETROOT AND SWEET POTATO WITH YOGHURT

MAKES ABOUT 1⅔ CUPS

• • • • • • • • • • • • • • • • • •

My toddler loves beetroot (beet), no doubt because he regularly ate beetroot purée as a baby. Beetroot's extraordinary bright colour is the clue that this vegetable is packed with potent nutrients, including plenty of antioxidants.

2 beetroot (beets), peeled and diced
1 small sweet potato, peeled and diced
1 tablespoon olive oil
2 tablespoons water or your baby's milk
1–2 tablespoons plain yoghurt

Preheat the oven to 200°C (400°F). Tear off a sheet of foil large enough to make a parcel for the vegetables and lay a sheet of baking paper on top. Place the beetroot and sweet potato in the centre, drizzle with olive oil and wrap up the parcel.

Place the parcel in a baking dish and roast for 35 minutes or until the vegetables are tender. Transfer the vegetables to a food processor with the water or milk. Blend to the desired consistency, adding a little more liquid if needed.

Set aside one serving and stir through the yoghurt. Freeze the remainder in individual portions for later use, adding fresh yoghurt just before serving.

* Suitable for freezing

'Root vegetables work wonderfully well in a mixed puree as they soften the flavour of stronger-tasting ingredients like beetroot and spinach.'

5

A WELL-ROUNDED DIET
10-12 MONTHS

YOUR BABY AT 10 MONTHS

By 10 months, your baby is probably a competent crawler and having a fabulous time exploring the world around him. He may even be pulling himself up to a stand and starting to cruise around the furniture, completely fascinated by all the new things he's discovering.

You can support his learning and natural curiosity by continuing to open up the amazing world of food and flavour to him. His sense of taste and touch are no less important than his other senses and, just as you might like to read him colourful books and play him music, you can also provide him with the most extraordinary stimulation through the food you put on his plate.

The key is variety – not just with flavour, but also texture. There's almost no limit to what you can give your baby now. Choking hazards and other prohibited foods aside (see pages 42 and 49), you should feel relaxed about letting your child try whatever food is on your plate. Don't worry if he hesitates or rejects it at first. Just seeing a fresh fig or some raspberries in his bowl and having a play with them and a little taste can be a really extraordinary experience for a baby. And – just like all his interactions with food – that experience will be carefully stored away in his amazing sponge-like brain and will contribute to the food choices he makes as he moves into his toddler years.

WHAT FOODS TO OFFER NOW

By the time your baby is 10 months, he should be having three meals a day, as well as the occasional snack when needed (see page 105). His meals should be getting more textured and he should also be getting plenty in the form of finger food. As his coordination improves, you'll probably notice your baby starts to become more skilled at eating with his fingers. He'll start to pick things up with greater confidence and become more capable at getting food into his mouth.

Importantly, your baby should be eating something from each of the major food groups – grains and cereals, vegetables and legumes, fruit, meat and eggs, and dairy – every day (see pages 12 to 15 for a detailed discussion, including a guide to serving sizes). Make sure he's having plenty of iron-rich foods. Because of their rapid growth, babies and toddlers are particularly vulnerable to iron deficiency (see page 18).

The meal planner opposite will give you a sense of how a balanced week of meals for a 10-month-old baby might look, using recipes from this book. Although it shows a wide variety of meals, which is ideal, you can repeat meals when you have leftovers or a batch of something in the freezer. And you may prefer to give your baby the same cereal for breakfast most mornings, perhaps with a different choice of fruit. Most of the time, your baby can just have a mashed or finger-food version of whatever you're eating.

This meal planner is simply a guide and you can use whatever system works for you. The planner presumes your baby is still on four breastmilk or formula milk feeds a day. However, some babies will be having three, or your baby may be having his milk at different times from those indicated, which is fine. Don't forget to offer your baby water after meals and throughout the day.

SAMPLE MEAL PLANNER FOR A 10-MONTH OLD

	Breakfast	Lunch	Mid-afternoon	Dinner	Bedtime
Day 1	Quick super porridge (page 106) Milk feed	Mini crustless quiches (page 111), steamed carrot sticks Milk feed	Milk feed	Tuna mornay pasta bake (page 121)	Milk feed
Day 2	Wholemeal crepes (page 108) with raspberries Milk feed	Chicken and pumpkin couscous (page 117) Milk feed	Milk feed	Farfalle with cauliflower and breadcrumbs (page 203)	Milk feed
Day 3	Fresh fruit with yoghurt and Blueberry sauce (page 145), toast fingers with avocado Milk feed	Beef, eggplant and mushroom ragù (page 118) with pasta Milk feed	Milk feed	Pumpkin and pea risotto (page 199)	Milk feed
Day 4	Multigrain French toast (page 107) with fruit purée Milk feed	Rolled risotto balls made from leftover Pumpkin and pea risotto (page 199) Milk feed	Milk feed	Lamb cutlets with three-vegetable mash (page 220)	Milk feed
Day 5	Banana and strawberry quinoa (page 79) Milk feed	Salmon cakes (page 113) Milk feed	Milk feed	Ratatouille (page 204)	Milk feed
Day 6	Quick super porridge (page 106) Milk feed	Chicken liver pâté (page 111) on toast fingers, cucumber sticks Milk feed	Milk feed	Fish and risoni stew (page 209)	Milk feed
Day 7	Herb scrambled eggs (page 110), serve of fruit Milk feed	Carrot, potato and zucchini frittata fingers (page 114) Milk feed	Milk feed	Melt-in-the-mouth beef casserole (page 218)	Milk feed

LEARNING TO SELF-FEED

It will be many months – perhaps not until she is two or even three years old – before your baby is able to feed herself using cutlery without your help, but until then, her hands make a terrific feeding tool. At about six months, babies tend to pick up small objects by using a raking motion with their hand and picking up the object in their fist. By around nine months, they start to develop a 'pincer grasp', which involves picking up an object between their thumb and forefinger. This is an exciting milestone for your baby because suddenly she can pick up small objects that have been causing her major frustration, like peas and corn kernels, quite efficiently. It also means you have to keep an eagle eye on her to make sure she's not putting all sorts of off-limits household items, like marbles and coins, in her mouth.

As her pincer grasp and coordination improve over the months, you'll start to notice your baby becomes much more adept at feeding herself. She'll also probably become a bit stroppier about you feeding her, preferring to take on this task all by herself. As well as using her hands, it's a good idea to let your baby have her own shorter-handled spoon, even as early as the time she starts solids. As painful as it is to watch a baby consistently miss her mouth and drop all her food in her lap, it is important to let her have a go. As with anything, if you always do it for her, she'll never learn. (I once knew a very capable 14-year-old boy who still passed his dinner plate to his mum so she could cut up his steak for him!)

Having said that, you also need to make sure your baby is getting some food in her mouth, so if she's having trouble, by all means help her out. Lots of parents continue to do the odd spoonfeeding well into the second year, so feel free to lend the occasional helping hand.

Other than giving your baby lots of different-shaped finger foods, an appropriate spoon and plenty of opportunity to have a go, there's not much you can do to accelerate the process of learning to self-feed. But loads of patience – and a big plastic bib – will certainly come in handy!

RELUCTANT SELF-FEEDERS

Babies who just want someone else to feed them are one of the less common concerns, and most parents have the reverse problem of their independent baby not letting them anywhere near her with a spoon. But, if your baby shows no interest in feeding herself, it may be that she needs to be shown what to do. The best way to teach her is to involve her in family mealtimes so that she can observe exactly how this whole business of feeding yourself works. Make sure you're also giving her plenty of different-shaped finger foods that she can hold with ease.

She may also be feeling some performance anxiety. Lots of babies like to have some time and space to enjoy their food, without Mum or Dad hovering over them. Although you shouldn't leave your baby on her own because of the choking risk, getting on with something else in the background while your baby has a chance to play with her lunch may create the pressure-free environment she needs to have a go.

BABY SNACKS

Snacks are a common part of most older babies' diets and you should certainly feel comfortable about giving them to your baby when you think he needs them, particularly during a growth spurt. However, because babies have such little appetites, it's easy for them to fill up on snacks and then miss one of their three meals or a milk feed. For this reason, you need to time snacks carefully. If you give them too close to lunch or dinner, chances are that your baby won't be interested in eating later on. The problem is that even a small snack can take the edge off your baby's hunger and end up replacing an entire, more substantial meal.

When you do give your baby a snack, you should try to make it just as healthy as the rest of his meals – a piece of fruit, some steamed vegetables, a cheese stick. That way, if he does end up missing lunch or dinner, it's no big deal. To my great delight, my son loved snacking on a little container of mixed legumes as a baby – red kidney beans, cannellini beans, borlotti beans and chickpeas. (I felt confident in his ability to eat them without choking, but their shape does make them a bit of a hazard, so watch out.)

As much as you might want to give your baby some of your chocolate cupcake, if only to enjoy the look of glee on his face, this is not a good habit to get into. Suddenly that container of legumes will seem decidedly boring by comparison!

FOOD – THE BEST POSSIBLE TOY

As a child, you were probably told a million times: 'Don't play with your food!' And now that you're a parent, you can probably understand why. Wouldn't it be wonderful if our children just ate their food without any fuss, and certainly without smearing it all over their faces, hands and highchairs?

Unfortunately for those of us left to clean up the mess, playing with food is actually a really important part of the process of learning how to eat and enjoy food. By squishing that piece of avocado all through his fingers and getting it all over his face, your baby is learning about the texture of avocado and what you need to do to get it into your mouth. He's also having a whole heap of fun doing it, which means he'll be saying to himself, 'Hey, this eating thing is pretty good. I really like it!'

Compare that with a baby who is fed only from a spoon and never allowed to touch anything – he probably dreads mealtimes and can't get out of his highchair fast enough when they're over.

So, although there's an awful lot of waste and mess that comes with it, encourage your baby to play with his food. Try not to stress if he gets it all over himself. In the long run, the dividends will pay off when you have a child who eats well, can adeptly feed himself and who loves his food.

QUICK SUPER PORRIDGE

MAKES 1 BABY SERVING

10–12 MONTHS

This super porridge takes moments to make and is so much better for your baby than a serve of most commercial breakfast cereals, which are often loaded with sugar and salt. You may need to adjust the quantities to match your baby's appetite.

If you want a higher-iron option, use a good-quality enriched baby porridge instead of the quick oats, and prepare it according to the instructions on the packet.

3 tablespoons quick porridge oats
1 tablespoon cube Frozen berry purée (page 107)
80 ml (3 fl oz/⅓ cup) boiling water
1 tablespoon plain yoghurt
¼ teaspoon chia seeds or LSA (or both)

Place the oats in a heatproof bowl with the frozen berry purée. Stir in the boiling water, then leave for 1 minute or until the purée has thawed.

Add the yoghurt and chia seeds or LSA and stir until the porridge is well combined.

WHY IS THIS PORRIDGE A SUPER BREAKFAST?

- **Oats** – nutrient rich and with a low glycaemic index (GI) for a slow energy release (see page 128). You don't have to make oat porridge every morning, though. There are many wonderful different grains you can try, such as rolled millet, amaranth, rye or quinoa.

- **Berries** – rich in iron, potassium, magnesium and folate, as well as vitamins A, C, E and the B vitamins. One of the highest-scoring fruits in terms of antioxidant content.

- **Chia** – a rich plant-based source of omega-3 fats, dietary fibre, protein and antioxidants.

- **LSA** – ground up linseeds, sunflower seeds and almonds. High in essential fats and other nutrients, and fantastic for your child's brain function. It is best not to cook LSA, as heat destroys the lovely omega-3 fats. Instead, stir it through your child's porridge at the last minute or simply sprinkle it on top.

- **Yoghurt** – make sure you choose a brand with live bacteria. Known as a 'probiotic', yoghurt will assist your baby's digestion and boost her immunity. Choose a full-fat variety until she is at least two years old. If your baby is accustomed to a sweeter breakfast, try replacing the plain yoghurt with fruit yoghurt until she accepts the new flavours.

FROZEN BERRY PURÉE

• • • • • • • • • • • • • • • • • • •

I like to have cubes of this purée in my freezer at all times. You can stir a cube through your child's porridge each morning (it will help to cool it down) or thaw it and stir it through yoghurt for dessert.

You can cook the berries in a bowl in the microwave if you prefer.

450 g (1 lb/3 cups) mixed frozen berries

Combine the berries and 125 ml (4 fl oz/½ cup) water in a saucepan. Cook over low heat until the berries are tender.

Blend the berries and cooking liquid until smooth. Freeze in individual portions.

* Suitable for freezing

MULTIGRAIN FRENCH TOAST

• • • • • • • • • • • • • • • • • • •

If you can't cope with yet another morning of fruit, cereal and yoghurt all over your baby's face, highchair and the floor, try this French toast. Cut into strips, it makes a delicious low-mess breakfast.

1 egg, lightly beaten
125 ml (4 fl oz/½ cup) milk
pinch of ground cinnamon
2 slices multigrain or wholemeal (whole-wheat)
    bread
1 teaspoon olive oil
Blueberry sauce (page 145) or a little fruit
    purée, to serve, optional

Mix the egg, milk and cinnamon in a shallow bowl. Soak each slice of bread in the egg mixture.

Heat the oil in a frying pan over medium–high heat. Fry the bread until golden brown on each side. Serve topped with a spoonful of blueberry sauce or fruit purée.

WHOLEMEAL CREPES

MAKES ABOUT 12

· • · •

Crepes make great finger food and they don't have to be a guilty pleasure. With wholemeal (whole-wheat) flour, three eggs and no sugar, you can feel quite virtuous about cooking these for your child. They are lovely served with blueberry sauce and fresh blueberries, instead of the traditional lemon and sugar.

You don't need to cook all of the crepes in one sitting. The batter will happily keep in an airtight container in the fridge for one or two days. If you have leftover cooked crepes, you can freeze them in a snaplock bag, separated by squares of plastic wrap (cling film), for another breakfast.

185 g (6½ oz/1¼ cups) wholemeal plain (whole-wheat all-purpose) flour
3 eggs
375 ml (12½ fl oz/1½ cups) milk
10 g (½ oz) butter, melted, plus extra, for cooking
Blueberry sauce (page 145) and fresh blueberries, to serve, optional

Sift the flour into a bowl. Make a well in the centre and add the eggs and milk. Start whisking the wet ingredients, gradually drawing in the flour until combined. Stir in the melted butter. If you have time, let the mixture stand for 1–2 hours or overnight.

Melt a little butter in a small or medium non-stick frying pan over medium heat. When the butter is bubbling, pour in enough batter to cover the base of the pan, and swirl to spread evenly. Cook the crepes for about 1 minute on each side or until golden.

Serve the folded crepes with the blueberry sauce and fresh blueberries.

* Suitable for freezing

HERB SCRAMBLED EGGS

MAKES 1 BABY SERVING + 2 ADULT SERVINGS

10–12 MONTHS

Eggs make a brilliant breakfast for your baby. They're a great source of protein, B vitamins and zinc. I buy organic eggs whenever possible, not only with the chicken's welfare in mind, but also because they can be more nutritious. Look for eggs from linseed-fed chickens, which will be rich in omega-3 fats.

3–5 eggs

15–30 g (½–1 oz) butter or 1 tablespoon olive oil

2–3 teaspoons finely snipped chives, parsley or basil

toast fingers, to serve

Break the eggs into a small bowl and beat together.

Melt the butter in a non-stick frying pan over medium heat. Add the eggs. Using a wooden spoon or a silicone spatula, stir the eggs slowly and gently until set.

Stir through the herbs and serve with toast fingers.

> **Vegetable scrambled eggs:** This is a good variation for boosting your baby's vegetable intake. Add the butter to the pan, then add ½ finely grated carrot and ½ finely grated zucchini (courgette). You can also add a couple of grated mushrooms. Cook for about 2 minutes or until soft, then add the eggs as per the recipe above. This also makes a super fast and wonderfully healthy lunch or dinner if you're time poor.

MINI CRUSTLESS QUICHES

MAKES 12

• ı • ı • ı • ı • ı • ı • ı • ı • ı • ı • ı • ı •

If the 'little trees' trick isn't working, encourage your baby to eat his broccoli with these seriously yummy quiches.

2 teaspoons olive oil
1 onion, finely diced
2 bacon rashers, diced
100 g (3½ oz) broccoli, finely chopped
60 g (2 oz/½ cup) grated cheddar cheese
4 eggs, lightly beaten
2 tablespoons milk
20 g (¾ oz) butter, melted

Preheat the oven to 180°C (350°F). Heat the oil in a frying pan over medium heat and cook the onion and bacon until almost soft. Add the broccoli and cook for a further 2 minutes. Divide the mixture among a 12-hole non-stick mini muffin tin. Top with the grated cheese.

Beat together the eggs, milk and melted butter until well combined. Divide the egg mixture evenly among the muffin holes and bake for about 15 minutes or until golden. Transfer to a plate to cool a little before serving.

CHICKEN LIVER PÂTÉ

MAKES ABOUT 2½ CUPS

• ı • ı • ı • ı • ı • ı • ı • ı • ı • ı • ı • ı •

Liver is one of the best sources of iron and a rich source of vitamin A. Because it is possible to have toxic amounts of vitamin A, you do need to watch that your child doesn't regularly eat large quantities of liver. A small serve of this pâté a couple of times a week is well within safe levels. Store it in the fridge for up to a week.

500 g (1 lb 2 oz) chicken livers
60 g (2 oz) butter
2 tablespoons chopped French shallots
sprig of thyme, leaves only
1 garlic clove, chopped
400 g (14 oz) can cannellini beans, drained
    and rinsed
juice of 1 orange

Remove any dark spots from the livers, and roughly chop. Melt half the butter in a large frying pan over medium heat. Gently cook the shallot until softened. Add the liver and thyme and increase the heat to high. Season with freshly ground black pepper (and, if you're making this for older children or yourself, a little salt too). Cook for 5 minutes, or until the liver is cooked through and browned, adding the garlic for the last 2 minutes.

Blend until smooth, then add the beans and process until smooth. Add the orange juice and process until shiny. Spoon into a terrine dish. Melt the remaining butter and pour over the pâté. Refrigerate until set.

SALMON CAKES

MAKES ABOUT 18

These salmon cakes make a great lunch when you're out and about, or they can be served warm with steamed vegetables or salad for dinner. If you have leftover fish, you can flake it and use it instead of the canned salmon.

The uncooked fish cakes can be frozen for later use. Simply thaw and cook them as needed.

500 g (1 lb 2 oz) potatoes (ebago or a
    similar variety), peeled and halved
1 garlic clove, peeled
20 g (¾ oz) butter
210 g (7 oz) can red salmon, drained,
    skin and bones retained
3 tablespoons grated parmesan
1 tablespoon finely snipped chives
3 tablespoons plain (all-purpose) flour
1 egg, lightly beaten
75 g (2½ oz/¾ cup) dry breadcrumbs
2 tablespoons light olive oil

Put the potato and garlic clove in a saucepan, cover with water and cook for 15–20 minutes or until tender. Drain, then return to the saucepan and cook over low heat for about 30 seconds or until dry. Remove from the heat and mash until smooth. Stir through the butter until it has melted. Set aside or refrigerate until completely cool.

Mix the salmon, parmesan and chives into the potato, carefully crushing the soft salmon bones as you go and ensuring there are no large chunks of salmon. Using your hands, form the mixture into 5 cm (2 in) patties.

Place the flour, egg and breadcrumbs in three separate shallow bowls. Dust the patties with flour, then dip into the egg, then coat with the breadcrumbs. Refrigerate for at least 1 hour.

Heat half the oil in a large frying pan over medium heat. Cook half the salmon cakes until golden brown on each side. Repeat with the remaining oil and salmon cakes. Drain on paper towels. Serve warm or cool.

* Suitable for freezing

> The soft bones found in canned salmon are a fantastic source of calcium. Crush them up so they cannot be detected by your baby.

CARROT, POTATO AND ZUCCHINI FRITTATA FINGERS

MAKES 24

The vegetables and eggs make these a well-balanced, nutritious finger food for your baby. Any older children in your family will love them too.

melted butter, for greasing
1 ½ tablespoons olive oil
80 g (3 oz/½ cup) grated carrot
80 g (3 oz/½ cup) grated potato or sweet potato
70 g (2½ oz/½ cup) grated zucchini (courgette)
2 spring onions (scallions), thinly sliced
1 tablespoon self-raising flour, sifted
6 eggs, lightly beaten
60 g (2 oz/½ cup) grated cheddar cheese
2 tablespoons finely chopped parsley

Preheat the oven to 180°C (350°F). Lightly grease a shallow 26 x 16 cm (6 x 10 in) cake tin with the melted butter. Line the base and two opposite sides with baking paper, allowing it to overhang.

Heat the oil in a saucepan over medium heat. Add the carrot and potato, and cook, stirring, for 3–4 minutes or until the vegetables soften. Add the zucchini and spring onion and cook for a further 3 minutes. Remove from the heat and set aside for 10 minutes to cool.

Combine the vegetable mixture, flour, egg, cheese and parsley in a large bowl and stir until well combined.

Spoon the vegetable mixture into the prepared tin and smooth the surface. Bake for 12 minutes or until set. Set aside for 10 minutes to cool. Lift the frittata from the tin and place on a plate to cool completely. Cut into fingers to serve.

CHICKEN AND PUMPKIN COUSCOUS

MAKES ABOUT 2 CUPS

By 10 months, your baby should well and truly be accustomed to more texture in her meals. If she's not, you can give this dish a little blend or mash, but try to make it lumpier over the coming weeks.

This makes a tasty, quick lunch that you and your baby can share if you like.

1 tablespoon olive oil

1 small onion, finely chopped

1 skinless chicken thigh fillet, trimmed and diced

50 g (2 oz/⅓ cup) diced pumpkin

125 ml (4 fl oz/½ cup) Chicken or Vegetable stock (page 190)

3 tablespoons instant couscous

1 teaspoon finely chopped coriander (cilantro) leaves or parsley, optional

Heat the olive oil in a saucepan over low–medium heat. Add the onion, chicken and pumpkin, cover and cook, stirring occasionally, for about 5 minutes or until the onion is soft.

Pour in the stock and bring to the boil. Reduce the heat and simmer for 8 minutes or until the pumpkin is tender.

Remove from the heat, stir in the couscous, cover and set aside for 6 minutes. Fluff with a fork and stir through the coriander or parsley.

One reason I always like to put herbs through my son's food (other than for the added nutrients) is so that he is used to seeing flecks of green on his plate. As parents, I think we should try to resist the temptation to 'dumb down' our children's meals. So far, my son has never kicked up a fuss about the green bits, because that's all he's ever known.

BEEF, EGGPLANT AND MUSHROOM RAGÙ

MAKES ABOUT 6 CUPS

· | · | · | · | · | · | · | · | · | · | · | · | · | · | · | · | · | · | · | · | · | · | · | · | · | · | · | · |

10–12 MONTHS

This is a delicious meal for every member of the family. Try it with minced (ground) lamb, or serve it on toast or with red kidney beans tossed through. It's also lovely for younger babies, blended to an appropriate consistency.

3 tablespoons olive oil
450 g (1 lb) minced (ground) beef or lamb
1 onion, finely chopped
1 eggplant (aubergine), peeled and diced
6 button mushrooms, thinly sliced
1 garlic clove, chopped
1 tablespoon plain (all-purpose) flour
400 g (14 oz) can no-added-salt chopped
    tomatoes
cooked pasta shapes, to serve

Heat 1 tablespoon of the oil in a deep frying pan or a saucepan over high heat. Brown the meat, breaking it up with a spoon as it cooks. Remove and set aside.

Add the remaining oil to the pan and cook the onion over medium–high heat for about 5 minutes or until soft. Reduce the heat, add the eggplant, mushrooms and garlic and cook for a further 5 minutes or until the onion is soft and the eggplant is golden.

Return the meat to the pan, stir through the flour, then add the tomatoes and 250 ml (8½ fl oz/1 cup) water. Bring to the boil, then reduce the heat, cover and simmer over low heat for 40 minutes. Depending on your baby's age and chewing development, you may wish to blend the sauce a little.

Set aside one serving and stir through the pasta. Freeze the remainder in individual portions for later use, stirring through freshly cooked pasta each time.

* Suitable for freezing

'While you're cooking, let your baby play with some of the ingredients. Let her touch the eggplant skin and teach her this new word. It's a crucial part of building her familiarity with a range of different foods.'

TUNA MORNAY PASTA BAKE

MAKES 8–10 BABY SERVINGS

You can freeze this in individual dishes for your baby and then thaw it as needed. Alternatively, serve it in a large dish for the whole family.

200 g (7 oz) small pasta shells
1 quantity cheesy béchamel sauce (see right)
425 g (15 oz) can tuna, drained and flaked
150 g (5 oz/1 cup) frozen peas
1 tablespoon finely chopped chives
50 g (2 oz/½ cup) grated parmesan or
    cheddar cheese
60–125 ml (2–4 fl oz/¼–½ cup) milk
80 g (3 oz/1 cup) fresh breadcrumbs
1 tablespoon olive oil

Preheat the oven to 200°C (400°F). Cook the pasta according to the instructions on the packet.

Stir together the pasta, béchamel sauce, tuna, peas, chives and half of the cheese until well combined. Add enough of the milk to make a soft creamy consistency. Spoon into individual ramekins.

Combine the breadcrumbs with the remaining cheese and the olive oil and sprinkle over the pasta. Bake for 15 minutes or until golden on top.

* Suitable for freezing

CHEESY BÉCHAMEL SAUCE

MAKES ABOUT 1½ CUPS

If you're having trouble getting your baby or toddler to eat his vegetables, a cheesy sauce like this one is bound to have him more interested. Just spoon a little over the top, or give it to him as a dipping sauce.

20 g (¾ oz) butter
2 tablespoons plain (all-purpose) flour
310 ml (10½ fl oz/1¼ cups) milk
60 g (2 oz/½ cup) grated cheddar cheese
pinch of grated nutmeg

Melt the butter in a small saucepan over low–medium heat. Add the flour and cook, stirring, for about 1 minute until the mixture combines to create a paste.

Gradually add the milk, stirring or whisking continuously. Keep stirring until the sauce becomes creamy and thick. Remove from the heat and stir in the cheese and nutmeg until well combined.

MINI APPLE, CINNAMON AND WALNUT MUFFINS

MAKES 36

Maple syrup adds a little sweetness to these delicious, moist muffins, but there is also plenty of goodness from the eggs, apple and nuts. They're certainly a whole lot healthier than any muffin you're likely to buy. Make sure you very finely chop the walnuts so that they don't pose a choking hazard.

Mini muffins are the perfect size for baby hands, but you can make regular-sized muffins if you don't have mini muffin trays. You can top the muffins with a little extra grated apple or finely chopped walnuts before baking.

2 eggs
3 tablespoons milk
125 ml (4 fl oz/½ cup) light olive oil or rice bran oil
2 tablespoons maple syrup
170 g (6 oz/1 cup) grated red or pink apple
40 g (1½ oz/⅓ cup) finely chopped walnuts
55 g (2 oz/½ cup) ground almonds
185 g (6½ oz/1¼ cups) self-raising flour
½ teaspoon ground cinnamon

Preheat the oven to 190°C (375°F). Grease three 12-hole mini muffin tins.

In a large bowl, stir together the eggs, milk, oil, maple syrup, grated apple, walnuts and almonds. Sift in the flour and cinnamon and gently stir until just combined. Spoon the mixture into the prepared muffin tins.

Bake for about 20 minutes or until the muffins are golden and cooked through. Stand in the tins for 5 minutes, then transfer to a wire rack to cool.

* Suitable for freezing

6

TODDLERS

FOOD AND YOUR TODDLER

The toddler years – typically described as between one and four years – are some of the most joyful and the most trying for parents. Your precious baby is now learning to walk and talk, and to assert her independence in no uncertain terms.

From an eating perspective, your toddler is likely to develop very strong opinions about every aspect of her meal – what she eats, what chair she sits in, what bib she wears (or doesn't wear), what spoon she uses . . . the list goes on.

Of course, how you choose to handle these battles will come down to your individual parenting style. Some parents will happily accommodate the demands of the toddler who will only eat dinner from her Peter Rabbit bowl, others will insist it's their way or the highway.

However, when it comes to your child's refusal to eat certain foods, it's important to know that many of the methods that might seem intuitive and that your parents might have used on you have now been proven to be counter-productive.

We now know that saying 'You can only have some ice cream if you eat your broccoli' is likely to make your child like broccoli even *less* and ice cream even *more*. Similarly, tactics such as 'You cannot leave the table until you finish your brussels sprouts' are most likely to produce a child with a lifelong hatred of brussels sprouts. The best strategies for dealing with eating struggles are covered in 'Fussy eating and food battles' on pages 132 to 137.

For new parents, rest assured that the toddler years are certainly not all doom and gloom when it comes to food. Compared with babies, toddlers are generally a lot more fun to have at the dinner table. You'll probably find it easier to involve them in family mealtimes and it is a total joy to watch them enjoying food, using cutlery and joining in the conversation.

What's more, there's a lot of fun to be had with your toddler in the kitchen. You can nurture a lifelong love of food and cooking by involving your child in simple tasks and explaining to her what you're doing – boiling the pot of water to cook the pasta, chopping the carrots and onions to make some soup – what may be mundane to you is utterly fascinating in the eyes of a curious toddler.

SUGAR IN YOUR TODDLER'S DIET

Now that your baby is over one year old, you can start to be a bit more relaxed about avoiding foods with added sugar. However, don't relax too much – although some sugar is part of a normal, healthy diet, ideally your toddler should have very moderate amounts.

Foods high in added sugar, like biscuits (cookies), cakes, ice cream and soft drinks, usually displace nutrient-dense foods in your toddler's diet. Your 18-month old had a chocolate muffin at four o'clock? I'm willing to bet he'll be much less interested in his vegetables and chicken when he sits down to dinner at six o'clock. While this is not a big problem if it happens from time to time, making a habit of it will definitely mean that your child misses out on a whole lot of nutrients that are very important for his physical and mental development. Foods high in added sugar provide lots of energy, but these are known as 'empty calories' because their nutrient content is usually hopelessly lacking.

Sugar and other energy-dense foods have a part to play in excess weight and the obesity epidemic that we're currently seeing in developed countries around the world. It breaks my heart to see a heavily overweight toddler because I know that he is likely to struggle with weight for the rest of his life.

Sugar can also cause tooth decay. The amount of damage depends on the form the sugar takes. Sticky foods, like toffees and dried fruits, stay on the teeth for longer, which means they produce more enamel-eroding acid in your child's mouth. The frequency of eating is also a factor. If your child eats four lollies in quick succession, his teeth will be exposed to far less acid damage than if he eats one lolly every half hour. This is why it's such a bad idea to let your child sip on a bottle of juice all day.

Yet another reason to limit sugar intake is that it can affect your child's behaviour. Eating sugary foods with a high glycaemic index (GI) will cause your child to experience a blood glucose high followed by a rapid drop in blood glucose levels, which may cause him to be irritable and lethargic (see page 128). That's why low-GI foods are a better option – they leave your child feeling fuller and more energetic for longer. However, some of the highest-GI foods, such as potatoes, have no added sugar, so the relationship between GI and added sugar is not always straightforward.

Eating sugary foods can also give your child a greater preference for sweet tastes. This can become a major nuisance for you when you're trying to encourage him to eat healthy, savoury foods, and can establish longer-term poor eating habits. Children are born with an innate preference for sweet tastes, but they gradually learn to like savoury and bitter tastes through repeated exposure to them. If your child's diet includes lots of sweet foods, he won't be getting as much of the critical exposure to non-sweet foods. He will also be learning that sweet treats are a regular part of his diet – not the message you want to be sending.

Having said this, I'm a firm believer in moderation and I do think that sweetness plays an important part in a joyful life. Some of my fondest childhood memories are coming home from school to a freshly baked cake being pulled from the oven, and cooking scones with my dad on a Sunday morning. It's just a matter of keeping sweet foods as treats, not staples, and making them as nutritious as possible – my apple and berry crumble with whole egg custard (page 229) is a perfect example.

WHITE SUGAR ALTERNATIVES

There are lots of sweet alternatives you can use instead of highly processed white sugar. They include honey (not suitable for children under one year because of the botulism risk), pure maple syrup, golden syrup and other cane sugars, such as soft brown and raw sugar. These alternatives tend to be marginally more nutritious than white sugar, because fewer of the nutrients have been stripped out, so I prefer to use them where possible. What's more, because they tend to be more flavoursome, I find you can use a little less.

In the case of brown sugar, some of the nutrient-rich molasses that has been removed from white sugar is typically added back in. Another alternative is rapadura sugar, which retains more vitamins and minerals than most other sugars. Like brown sugar, it should only be used where the colour of your baking is not critical. You can also buy low-GI sugar, which has a GI of around 50 (instead of 65–70) and also contains slightly more nutrients than white sugar.

While these alternatives are great, don't be fooled into thinking that they're some kind of health food. Ultimately they are similar to white sugar, although a bit less refined and more nutritious.

A WORD ON GLYCAEMIC INDEX (GI)

When your child eats carbohydrates, his digestive system breaks them down into glucose (and other simple sugars), which gets released into his bloodstream and provides much-needed fuel to his active muscles and brain. The glycaemic index (GI) is a scale used to compare carbohydrates according to how they affect the glucose levels in our blood. Foods with a high GI rating convert into glucose quickly and produce a rapid spike in blood glucose levels, whereas foods with a low GI break down more slowly, producing a more constant release of glucose into the bloodstream.

As a general rule, it's best if your child's diet includes plenty of low-GI foods and smaller amounts of high-GI foods. When your child eats a low-GI meal, like a breakfast of oat porridge and yoghurt, he will have a good, constant energy release, which means his brain will receive a steady flow of fuel and he'll find it easier to learn new things. He'll also be more motivated to play and climb for a longer time, which is so important for his development.

On the other hand, when he eats a high-GI meal, like puffed white rice cereal and white toast, he has a sugar high and then, within an hour or two, his blood glucose and energy levels plummet, making it hard for him to concentrate. He'll probably become cranky and no longer enjoy playing, and will crave sweet or fatty food for a quick energy boost.

Over time, it is believed that the efforts of your child's body to moderate the highs and lows of his blood glucose levels may be damaging to his blood vessels and nerves. High-GI foods are also associated with overeating and weight gain, and may be linked to diabetes and heart disease.

'Glycaemic load' (GL) is a measurement that takes into account the amount of carbohydrate present in the food, which also affects blood glucose levels. For example, pumpkin has a relatively high GI, but doesn't contain much carbohydrate, so its GL is quite low, making it a good, healthy option. You can find a large online database of GI and GL values at www.glycemicindex.com.

SALT IN YOUR TODDLER'S DIET

Having been through your baby's first year, you already know that it's important not to add salt to baby foods. A baby's developing kidneys simply can't process much salt, which is why too much can cause serious dehydration and, in very extreme cases, even prove fatal.

The situation doesn't change much in the toddler years and a low-salt diet – no more than 2 grams per day – is recommended. But being careful with the salt shaker won't necessarily do the trick. It has been estimated that about 75 per cent of our salt intake is from manufactured foods, with only 25 per cent coming from the salt added during cooking and at the table. For example, two slices of commercial bread typically contain 1 gram of salt – half your child's recommended intake. Other high-salt culprits are commercial soups, sauces (including pasta sauces and soy sauces), pizzas, dips, breakfast cereals, crisps, biscuits (cookies), sausages, burgers, some cheeses and anything with added flavourings, like instant noodles.

There are really good reasons to take salt intake seriously. Eating lots of salt raises blood pressure, even in children. This, in turn, increases the risk of cardiovascular disease and stroke – both of which are potential killers. There is also evidence of a possible link between high salt intake and stomach cancer and even osteoporosis, because salt causes an increase in calcium excretion. Given how straightforward it is to minimise the salt in your child's (and your) diet, you'd be crazy not to do it.

READING FOOD LABELS

You'll notice that food labels list 'sodium' in the nutritional information panel, rather than salt. It's useful to know that 400 mg of sodium equals 1 gram of salt. Your toddler shouldn't have more than about 800 mg of sodium a day.

When choosing packaged foods, go for low-salt options, ideally less than 120 mg of sodium per 100 grams. If the label says that the product has more than 600 mg per 100 grams, you're in high-salt territory – spare your child and yourself from all those potential health problems and put it back on the shelf, or eat small quantities.

CUT THE SALT . . . BUT WATCH THE IODINE

One thing you do need to watch out for when you're reducing your child's salt intake is that she's still getting enough iodine – an essential mineral that all children need for proper thyroid function and for optimal cognitive development and motor function. In fact, the World Health Organization has found that iodine deficiency is one of the main worldwide causes of impaired cognitive development in children.

Although salt is not a naturally high source of iodine, much of the salt consumed throughout the world is fortified with iodine, following government initiatives to improve population iodine levels. In Australia and New Zealand, it is now mandatory for all commercial breads (except organic and salt-free breads) to use iodised salt, making bread an important source of iodine for children in these countries. In the UK and US bread fortification is not mandatory, but bread manufacturers can use iodised salt if they wish.

Because iodine is such a critical nutrient, you do need to make sure that your child is still getting plenty if she's not eating much iodised salt. Other good sources include seafood, seaweed and eggs. If your child is on a low-salt vegan diet, you might like to consider using an iodine supplement.

A WORD ON SALT AND HEART HEALTH

I have a friend who adds bucket-loads of salt to every meal. He says he doesn't like the taste of his food without it. Not surprisingly, he had a heart attack at the age of 46. Thankfully, he recognised the signs that it was coming and managed to get himself to a hospital moments before it occurred, which ended up saving his life. One thing I find fascinating is that he says his mum always added lots of salt to her cooking when he was a little boy. It appears that she might have set the stage for his lifelong love affair with salt.

My friend's experience is consistent with some research done by the US Monell Chemical Senses Center, arguably the world's leading research institute in the field of taste preferences. They have found that young babies exposed to salt are more likely to have a higher preference for salty tastes, both at six months of age and into their pre-school years. So, feeding a baby high-salt foods appears to create a salt-loving older child and – although we need further research to know this for sure – possibly a salt-loving adult.

Through other research, we also know that when it comes to salt, regardless of your childhood experiences, the more you eat, the more you want. Due to the turnover of taste receptor cells in humans, our taste system is flexible and responsive to environmental changes. Studies have shown that adults placed on low-sodium diets become more sensitive to salty tastes and, over time, have a decreased liking of salty foods. Similarly, those exposed to high salt concentrations end up having an increased liking of salty foods. If you're in any doubt, you can run your own experiment. Put yourself on a low-salt diet and soon enough you'll see how it lowers your tolerance for salty foods. I promise your body will thank you for the change.

All this is fantastically empowering for you as a parent. By limiting your child's salt intake now, you might well be shaping her adult taste preferences for less salty food, which might just end up saving her life. You'll also be putting her at far less risk of high blood pressure during her childhood years and possibly into adulthood – yet another reason to cut the salt.

FUSSY EATING AND FOOD BATTLES

The term 'fussy eating' or 'picky eating' is usually used to describe the behaviour of children who will eat only a small variety of food. In more serious cases, it may be just a few ingredients. Fussy eaters are typically unwilling to try new foods (this is called food 'neophobia') and are also usually unwilling to eat many of the foods that they have seen, perhaps even eaten, before. Often fussy eaters won't eat anything from an entire food group, such as dairy, vegetables or meat.

It is rare to have a child who doesn't experience some food fussiness at least once in his childhood. My son is a great eater, on the whole. Some days he will happily eat raspberry quinoa porridge for breakfast and osso bucco for lunch. But I would be lying if I said he hasn't had some absolutely shocking days when it comes to food. These days will come, and hopefully go, and it is a matter of getting through them as calmly as possible. It's when the days start to turn into weeks and months of unhealthy eating that you have a problem.

Worryingly, fussy eating can result in serious nutritional deficiencies and can also cause major stress for the whole family. Thankfully, there are a whole lot of concrete steps you can take to try to prevent your child from becoming a fussy eater, and to stop things from getting any worse if he does.

PREVENTING FUSSY EATING

The easiest way of dealing with fussy eating is to try and avoid it in the first place. If your child is under 12 months (or even two years), you have a golden opportunity to set the stage for healthy eating behaviours. It is helpful to understand how your baby's taste preferences develop and the role you play in shaping that process (pages 27 to 29 have a detailed discussion of taste preferences). By following some simple steps, including repeatedly exposing your baby to a large range of different flavours, building his familiarity with different ingredients, and helping him to manage all sorts of different textures, you will be well on the way to avoiding fussy eating down the track.

Having said that, there are no guarantees as a parent, and despite your best efforts you may end up with the world's trickiest eater. Hard as it is, you should definitely not see this as a reflection of your parenting. Sometimes, medical conditions (perhaps undiagnosed) are at play (see page 138). Other times, for no apparent reason, your child is simply one of those who just isn't interested in food. If this happens, don't give up. There is still plenty you can do to stop your child's eating from getting worse over time.

To make sure Aoibhe is hungry for mealtimes, we don't give her any snacks after 11 a.m. or 4 p.m. I think it's unfair to expect a kid to enjoy mealtimes if they're half full already.

At mealtimes, I always put a range of different vegetables and meat on her plate, even if I know full well she won't eat some of them. I never pick out her favourite bits to give her. She can leave them behind if she wants, but she gets to see them on her plate every time. I have been surprised at the number of times she chooses to just eat them.

Claire, mother of Aoibhe (2).

HANDLING A FUSSY TODDLER

Having a child who is a seriously fussy eater can make your life miserable. Instead of sitting down and enjoying a lovely home-cooked dinner each night, you're going into battle. Your toddler refuses to eat a single thing on his plate, he shakes his head, demands another meal, maybe even throws his dinner on the floor. There are tears (probably yours), perhaps an argument with your partner, and yet another night of an entire meal ending up in the bin. You're so worried about your child not eating enough, you end up resorting to jam (jelly) on white toast for the fifth night in a row. And even then your child will only eat if the television is on. You can now count on one hand the ingredients he'll eat, none of which are green.

If this sounds familiar, rest assured that you're not alone. In a US survey of over 3000 children, 50 per cent of caregivers (mainly mothers) reported that their 19- to 24-month-old toddler was a picky eater. However, the fact that it's common doesn't make it any less stressful for you and I bet you'd be willing to try almost anything if it meant you could have even one harmonious family dinner where your toddler just ate the food you served him without complaint.

One thing that may comfort you is knowing that there has been lots of scientific research done into fussy eating in recent years and we now know a lot more about which approaches do and don't work. Interestingly, we now know that most of the tactics our parents used on us – 'You can't leave the table until you finish what's on your plate', 'No dessert unless you eat your vegetables', 'If you don't eat those brussels sprouts, you'll be getting them for breakfast' – are counterproductive and actually tend to make matters worse.

In a nutshell, the research findings tell us that the best approach for minimising fussy eating is simply to keep serving up healthy varied foods, avoid all coercive behaviours and be a good role model by eating well yourself. Some of the key strategies are outlined below.

Offer a range of healthy foods, even if your child doesn't like them One of the key predictors of whether or not a child will eat a certain food is familiarity. Basically, children eat what they like and they like what they know. If your child has only seen or tasted a food a few times, you can hardly expect it to be his favourite. One problem that typically arises with fussy eaters is that their parents end up only serving the few ingredients they'll eat. As their list of 'liked foods' starts to narrow, so too does their parents' shopping list and before long, they're eating only three things – all of which are white carbohydrates. It is very difficult to get out of this rut if you don't continually challenge your child's fussiness by putting different foods on his plate. If he has a meltdown because the peas are touching his other favourites, put them in a separate bowl. Just don't stop serving them.

Eat a range of healthy foods yourself Don't underestimate the power of your actions on your child. Your child's sponge-like brain is soaking up your every move and using that as the basis for his own behaviour. A number of studies around the world have found the diet of a child's mother to be particularly important. In fact, the number of vegetables liked by a child's mother has been found to be a reliable predictor of the vegetable variety consumed by the child. But dads are important too, particularly when it comes to what their sons will eat. This is one reason it's great if your child can eat with you as a family – the more he sees you eating up your vegetables, the more likely he is to do the same.

Don't stress about quantities There is a really good reason that most books don't give precise quantities for how much your baby or toddler should be eating. The reality is that children of the same age and gender eat wildly varying amounts. There are all sorts of reasons your child may have a smaller or larger appetite than his

HOW DO YOU GET A FUSSY EATER TO 'HAVE A TRY'?

I realise that it's all well and good to say to encourage your child to try a new food, but how do you actually do this? Believe me, I've battled with the same issue myself plenty of times. It's most frustrating when you believe that if your toddler would just have a taste, he would really like what you're offering.

I had this experience when I gave my son a lychee. Because he had no idea what it was, there was no way he was going to start munching on it. Yet, being a fan of other sweet fruits, I felt sure that he would love it if only he would have a try. So, I tried turning it into a sort of game. I gave him an unpeeled lychee and asked him to try to get the skin off and the pip out, demonstrating on my own lychee. He soon became immersed in this task and, having tasted the juice running down his fingers, he eventually followed my lead in having a little try. I think letting him play with the whole fruit for a while helped him to overcome any fear of this strange food and finally have a taste.

This is just one of a hundred strategies you could try. Some others are listed below.

- Sit your toddler at the dinner table with a few other people and start a 'copy cat' game – this is one I've had great success with. Start by asking everyone at the table to eat one or two things you know your toddler likes. Everyone eats in unison and there's a great cheer. Then move on to the food your toddler won't try and say, 'OK everyone, let's eat some green beans!' Everyone picks up their bean and starts munching. If your toddler, like mine, hates missing out on anything, he's bound to follow suit.

- Sing a song or tell a story about the food in question.

- Ask an older child who your toddler admires to eat some in his presence.

- Put a small piece of the food next to a selection of familiar, liked foods. Sometimes in the context of an otherwise normal meal, something new can slip under the radar.

- Involve your toddler in the gardening or cooking process – there is research that suggests that children are more inclined to try foods that they've grown or cooked themselves.

- Distract your child while he has his first taste. This kind of covert strategy is not one I usually advise but it can make the world of difference. There have been a few times that my son has started eating an entirely new food because I managed to give him a little mouthful when he was a bit distracted. Although I really prefer to keep my mobile phone well away from mealtimes, showing your child a quick photo or video clip while he has his first taste and then taking it away for the rest of the meal can get him over the initial taste hurdle. Once that's crossed, he might happily continue on his own.

- For an older child, you could try a rewards chart. Just make sure the reward isn't another food, and make sure you're rewarding just having a taste. The chart shouldn't involve your child having to eat a whole plateful, as this interferes with his ability to self-regulate the amounts he eats.

peers on any given day, including whether or not he's having a growth spurt, is teething, tired or unwell, and how much he's eaten at other meals that day. That's why it's much better to be guided by your child's growth than his serving sizes. There is now good evidence that being relaxed about how much your child eats is more likely to result in healthy eating behaviours and less likely to result in tension and stand-offs between the two of you at mealtimes. A useful guiding motto is that you as the parent choose the quality (what food is served) and your child chooses the quantity.

What if your child has only eaten two mouthfuls? That's fine. Of course, you wouldn't want that happening every meal, but from time to time children won't eat much, and trying to force them to have more will only make matters worse. Having said that, if the sparrow-style eating persists, you may have to investigate any possible medical problems.

Don't say 'finish everything on your plate' There is research that suggests that babies and toddlers have a very good inherent ability to regulate their own appetites. They know to eat when they're hungry and they know to stop eating when they've had enough. However, years of being told to eat everything on their plate interferes with this and can create an adult with a 'plate clearing' mentality and a serious weight problem. Encouraging your child to be guided by his own hungry and full signs sets him up for a really healthy relationship with his own body and its needs. Some days your child will need far more than you put on his plate, some days he'll need far less. If you force your child to clear his plate, you may turn a child who would otherwise be a perfectly content little eater into one who resents mealtimes, and you.

Serve your child's meal when he's hungry From my experience, sitting your child down to a meal when he's not hungry is one of the biggest mistakes parents (including myself) commonly make. We prepare a beautiful meal, we sit our child down to eat it and we get upset when he doesn't want any. Before you have your own toddler meltdown, stop and think about his day. How many snacks has he had? How much milk? How much juice? Although toddlers typically do need little snacks to get them through the day, if they've had a bowl of crackers or a smoothie at 4.30 p.m., of course they're not going to be interested in dinner at 5.30 p.m. I find it absolutely extraordinary how my son's hunger dictates what he'll eat. If he's hungry, he'll eat just about anything – broccoli, pumpkin, cauliflower, spinach, steak, fish, casseroles, soups, even a totally new ingredient he's never seen before. Nothing's off the menu. But, if he's had a big snack in the last couple of hours, forget about it. Only pasta, bread and cheese will do.

When Zac was around 18 months, he started rejecting a lot of food and sometimes refused to eat altogether. We soon realised there was a lot of stress around mealtimes and pressure on him to eat. I was inconsistent about when and where he ate, and would place a mountain of food in front of him and stare at him anxiously, willing him to eat it.

So we tried to remove the anxiety and make mealtimes predictable and fun. He now eats at his toddler table at the same time each day. I give him a fun colourful plate with a variety of brightly coloured finger foods on it, and let him decide what he wants to eat. Since it's become an adventure where he feels in control and not under pressure, he's eating a whole lot more in terms of volume and variety.

Amy, mother of Zachary (2).

However, the problem is that calculating your child's hunger is a very delicate balancing act. Unlike adults, children can't go hungry for very long before they lose the plot, have a meltdown, and refuse to eat altogether. So the trick is to catch your child when he's hungry, but not at breaking point. This is not always easy to manage – particularly when you have two or more kids – and there are times we all get it wrong. But ensuring that snacks are small and not too filling, watching out for big drinks and trying to catch that 'sweet spot' during the day when your child is hungry but not starving can make the world of difference to his fussiness. Serving meals at similar times each day can also really help as it gets your child into the rhythm of regular, predictable meals.

Don't hide all of your child's vegetables As discussed above and on pages 28 and 29, familiarity is one of the key indicators determining whether or not a child will eat a particular food. In order to be familiar with a food, your child needs to know he's eating it. So if he only ever eats broccoli when it's puréed and stirred through spaghetti bolognese, of course he's not going to be tempted to pick up a floret and start munching on it. Hiding vegetables is an excellent way to improve the diet of a fussy eater. But – and it's a big but – it's critical that your child also sees vegetables in their whole form, even if you're dead sure he won't eat them that way. By all means, purée and hide to your heart's content, just include a side of beans and cauliflower too. Your child needs to learn what vegetables look like and how they taste in their whole form. He also needs to learn that vegetables are an important part of most meals and he won't be getting that message if they're always hidden.

Don't pressure your child to eat This is a really hard one and requires mountains of patience. It means not saying to your child, 'You can't watch TV unless you eat three more mouthfuls'. It means not saying, 'It would make Mummy/Daddy really happy if you ate up your steak'. And it certainly means not saying, 'You can't leave the table until you finish your dinner'. Research tells us that the problem with these kinds of strategies is that they simply don't work. In the short term, your child may finish his plate of fish when he otherwise would have walked away, but in the long term, he's less likely to eat fish and more likely to try and manipulate you at mealtimes. If your toddler gets the sense that you really, really care about what and how much he eats, he's probably going to realise it's an easy way to get some control over you. Not that I'm suggesting your precious child has Machiavellian motives, but the reality is that lots of toddlers learn that by being a difficult eater they can get lots of attention from their parents, along with some pretty cool rewards. However, if you're relaxed about your child's food intake, mealtimes are far less likely to become a battleground where you and your toddler go head-to-head.

Encourage your child to 'have a try' While pressuring your child to eat is generally counterproductive, it is fine to encourage your toddler to have a little 'try' or a 'taste' of different foods. But it's important to distinguish between a taste and having to eat the whole bowl. It's also important to distinguish between encouragement and coercion or pressure. So while you might say, 'Why don't you taste the papaya? I think it's really yummy', this is very different from making your child sit in his chair until he finishes the whole bowl. The key is that if your child doesn't want to have a try, you shouldn't have a flip out. Just stay calm and don't press the issue. Try serving it again another day.

Don't reward food with food 'If you eat your peas, you can have some yummy chocolate cake!' Sounds like a good deal. What's more, it will probably work. Peas eaten, mission accomplished. If only it were that simple. Unfortunately, we now know that this strategy is likely to make your child like peas even less, and chocolate cake even more. And it's not hard to see why. From your child's perspective, peas are suddenly a chore, a task, a dreaded thing you have to get through, and cake is a special treat, a deluxe reward. If you want your child to eat peas, serve them to him regularly, make mealtimes a positive experience and eat peas yourself. Just don't offer him any cake for his efforts.

Keep mealtimes fun I'm not suggesting that you have to turn into some kind of circus performer, but the truth is that children form a liking or a disliking for foods depending on their mealtime associations. For example, I have a 55-year-old friend who won't drink milk. Why? Because as a child she was forced to drink a carton of lukewarm milk at school every day. She wasn't allowed to leave her desk until she finished it. Over time, this gave her a very negative association with milk and now it makes her physically ill to even think about drinking it. The same applies in reverse. If your child's experience of mealtimes is positive and conflict-free, according to the research in this field, he's going to be more likely to form a liking for the foods you serve him. Just think of your own favourite or least-liked dish – there's probably a memory or experience that made it so. This is yet another reason why it's not a good idea to enter into a stand-off with your child over food. If you pressure him to eat a particular ingredient, he's just going to end up hating it. But if dinner is served with a few laughs, and no-one seems to care what he eats, there's no reason for him to develop food aversions.

Be strict on your shopping, not on your child Poor old parents, it seems we can do nothing right. The weight of research now suggests that the more restrictions you put on your child's consumption of a particular food, the more likely he is to want that food. The forbidden fruit – as it turns out, does taste better. However, it's important to distinguish between types of restriction. The kind of restriction that ultimately works against you is when you tell your toddler that he's never allowed any of the chocolate biscuits (cookies) that are sitting in full view on the kitchen shelf. However, it appears that adopting a less direct style of 'prudent restriction', namely not having any chocolate biscuits in the house in the first place, doesn't backfire in the same way. The research suggests that the best approach is to be strict on your shopping list – keeping unhealthy foods to a minimum – but when those foods are in your house (and your toddler knows about them), don't overly restrict his access to them. You could see this as an opportunity to clean up your own bad eating habits. Time to stop buying those packets of potato chips!

Don't call your child a 'fussy eater' Most parents tend to be pretty good at putting labels on their child, particularly when there's a sibling or two. When you were growing up, maybe you were the clever one, the naughty one or the sporty one. Perhaps you were the good eater or possibly the dreaded fussy eater! The problem is that pigeon-holing a child in this way can make him think that he can't or shouldn't change his ways. Or, worse still, he might actually like the attention that goes with the label and become more entrenched in his behaviour.

Knowing how important it is that my son has good eating role models, I have sometimes found it useful to get his toys in on the action. Since he was a baby, I have occasionally brought his favourite teddy to the table so that Teddy could also enjoy some of his meals. As it turns out, Teddy is a particular fan of green beans, beetroot (beet) and tomatoes. In fact, he eats them with such gusto that we sometimes have to remind him to be a good sharer and save some for us. Occasionally, I give my son another spoon or fork so that he can feed Teddy himself. Try it for yourself, but my experience has been that if my son sees his trustworthy bear 'enjoying' something he's a bit unsure about, he's been much more willing to give it a go himself.

MEDICAL CONDITIONS THAT CAN AFFECT YOUR CHILD'S EATING

If your child is struggling with textured foods, being fussy about particular ingredients or refusing to eat altogether, there may well be a medical issue at play. If the behaviour persists, it's a good idea to get it investigated instead of assuming that she's just being headstrong, because some problems do get worse over time. Below are some of the more common medical causes of eating problems.

REFLUX

Gastro-oesophageal reflux is relatively common in babies and there would be few parents who haven't had to deal with a milk feed coming back up all over their clothes and carpet. However, in the case of severe reflux, which affects only a small minority of children, more serious feeding problems can arise. In particular, babies with severe reflux may have real difficulty coping with textured, lumpy foods. If your baby is still favouring smooth purées and showing an aversion for lumps after her first birthday, it's quite possible that reflux or some other medical issue is responsible and you should have her checked out by your doctor or paediatrician.

CONSTIPATION

When children are constipated, their stomachs may not empty properly because things have come to a standstill further down in their digestive system. This can affect their appetite and cause them to refuse food. You'll know if your child is constipated because her poo will be dry and pebbly instead of soft. There are a number of reasons your child may be constipated, including if she's recently started solids, if she's not getting enough insoluble fibre (found in vegetables, fruits – preferably skin on – and whole grains), and if she's not getting enough water. Although it's a fluid, milk is not the same as water and too much can make matters worse. Prunes and prune juice are a great help when you have a constipated toddler, although don't go overboard as they can have a pretty powerful effect!

If her appetite doesn't return after the constipation has resolved, there may be other medical issues that need to be investigated.

TEETHING

As important as they are, teeth can be a serious nuisance to parents of babies and toddlers. There always seems to be one coming up, giving your child (and you) grief. Common symptoms associated with teething include red cheeks, dribbling, gum rubbing, biting, ear tugging or rubbing, nasal congestion, disturbed sleep, irritability, crying, fever, diarrhoea and loss of appetite. Children who have serious tooth pain may not want to eat at all, preferring just to have milk or smooth purées. While this is fine for a day or two, you will need to encourage your child to get back to her normal eating regime as soon as her teeth can manage it so that she doesn't decide she wants to move to a liquid diet permanently. Resist any temptation to put rice cereal or other food in your baby's bottle. There is a risk of choking and dental decay, and it can lead to longer-term feeding problems.

CHEWING AND SWALLOWING PROBLEMS

Between the ages of six and 24 months, your baby's mouth is going through a phenomenal learning process. Although you will probably be unaware of the subtleties, her facial muscles, tongue and jaw are all developing at a rapid rate and learning how to chew and, eventually, talk. For many children, this process unfolds quite naturally without any particular help from their parents, other than exposure to an increasingly varied range of food textures. However, for some children, learning to chew and swallow food is not so straightforward and you may have to take texture changes very gradually. Some children will find it much easier to chew on finger foods, like rusks, than lumpy purées, and most seem to prefer food that is coarse-textured throughout rather than runny with an occasional big lump.

If your child is really struggling with texture compared with her peers and you're having trouble feeding her anything other than smooth purées, it is worth getting her checked by your doctor or a speech pathologist, as there may be an underlying medical cause.

TONSILS AND ADENOIDS

The days of removing children's tonsils for no apparent good reason are long gone, and most of us now get through life without our tonsils giving us any trouble at all. However, some children do unfortunately experience enlarged or infected tonsils, which will almost certainly interfere with their eating. A child with sore tonsils will probably feel pain each time they swallow and, if the tonsils are infected, they may have pus coming from them, which will likely taste awful. Because of the pain, a child with enlarged tonsils will probably prefer soft foods or nothing at all.

Children with enlarged adenoids will also find eating difficult, because they typically need to breathe through the mouth, which makes mealtimes an exhausting juggling act for their mouth. Not surprisingly, research has shown that children suffering from enlarged adenoids and tonsils are at greater risk of being underweight.

FOOD ALLERGY AND INTOLERANCE

In many cases of food allergy and intolerance (discussed on pages 30 to 32), parents are acutely aware of their child's sensitivity and know to keep the culprit foods off the menu. However, some cases do not present with obvious external symptoms and instead parents may think their child is just a problem feeder. For example, babies with cow's milk protein allergy might be experiencing considerable discomfort for some time before a diagnosis is made. Children with a food intolerance or allergy may have stomach cramping or bloating, which will not necessarily be apparent to their parents but which is likely to interfere with their eating.

INTRODUCING YOUR TODDLER TO THE KITCHEN

Bringing a toddler into the kitchen can turn a simple meal into a large-scale cooking production involving every bowl you own and a mess resembling a disaster zone. It's no surprise that most of us try to get the job done while our toddlers are nicely distracted.

As tempting as it is to shoo him out of the kitchen, letting your toddler lend an occasional helping hand is a vital part of teaching him about the wondrous world of food and cooking. I find it astounding the extent to which parents' cooking habits shape their children. Of my own friends, all the best cooks have come from families interested in food, and those who can't cook always say their parents didn't know how. Given how important cooking is for our health and quality of life, sending your grown child out into the world knowing how to cook is just about the best gift you could give him.

Here are some tips to help make the experience positive for you both:

- **Early days –** before your child is old enough to help with stirring and measuring, you can start his love affair with cooking by letting him be the audience in your very own live cooking show. Your child's extraordinary brain soaks up your every move and he is able to learn an awful lot just from watching and listening. So make sure you fill him in on what you're up to. As he sits in his highchair, explain to him that you're dicing the onions to make risotto and stirring the custard to make it smooth. Give him a wooden spoon and an upturned saucepan to beat and let him play with a whisk and some measuring cups. Pop him on your hip as you stir the béchamel sauce and explain how it thickens with time. A lot will go over his head, but he'll still be taking plenty on board and having lots of fun at the same time.

- **Budding sous chef –** from about 18 months, you can start to involve your toddler in some basic cooking tasks. There will be major mess, but activities like stirring batter, rolling out dough, icing cupcakes and cutting out sandwich shapes are seriously fun for a little person. The key is to have plenty of time and zero expectations. It's all about the process, not the finished product. As painful as it is to watch a toddler's clumsy efforts, resist the temptation to take over. Teach him by demonstrating alongside with your own rolling pin and ball of dough rather than taking over his.

- **Knife skills –** obviously, handing a kitchen knife to a toddler is absolutely out of the question. Thankfully, you can buy child-friendly knives that will cut a carrot, but not your child's hand. Of course, you'll still need to watch that your child doesn't poke himself in the eye, but now that my son has his special knife, helping me with chopping is one of his favourite kitchen pastimes.

- **Making a meal –** by the time your toddler is about three, he can start to follow a recipe with you and together you can make a favourite dish from scratch. This is when the fun really begins, as your toddler will soon learn that cooking involves a series of steps that, when followed properly, have a delicious result. The sense of pride and achievement that comes with making his very own dish that everyone in the family can eat is really quite special. For a more timid child, it can be a great confidence booster. Choose recipes that offer fairly instant gratification, like smoothies, fruit sticks, sandwiches, pizzas or muffins.

- **Maths and science –** one benefit of involving your toddler in the kitchen is that he will be learning some key foundations of maths and science as part of the process. Measuring, adding, fractions, volumes, chemistry – they're all part of basic baking. While you don't want a fun afternoon of making cookies to turn into a maths lecture, you can feel particularly virtuous knowing that a batch of brownies is helping to prepare your toddler for school.

- **A signature dish –** as your child gets older and becomes reasonably competent in the kitchen, encourage him to have 'signature dishes'. Make these dishes with him as many times as it takes for him to know them by heart and be able to make them on his own. They should be different from the dishes his siblings make so that he has a sense of ownership of them. This can give your child confidence and set him up for a lifetime of feeling at home in a kitchen.

A WORD ON TODDLER DRINKS

Your toddler should be drinking about 250 ml (8½ fl oz/1 cup) of milk per day (more if she's not eating other sources of calcium), plenty of water, and nothing else. Here's why:

- **Not too much milk –** milk is a really important source of calcium for your toddler's growing bones. However, having too much milk can put your toddler at risk of iron deficiency. Children who are 'milkoholics' tend to fill up on milk, which is low in iron, and then have no appetite for other iron-rich foods. Don't let your toddler have a big glass of milk or a smoothie before dinner. There's just no way her little tummy will manage a proper meal when it's full of milk.

- **Not too much juice –** juice should be a treat, not a staple. Drinking too much juice can cause all sorts of toddler problems, including diarrhoea, tooth decay and iron deficiency. I find it's easiest not to have juice in the house. Instead, my son has it as an occasional treat when we're out. However, if you've got a seriously fussy eater who won't touch fruit or vegetables, having your own juice press might just allow you to get the odd carrot, beetroot (beet), apple and orange into her.

- **No soft drinks –** there is no good reason to get your toddler into the habit of drinking soft drinks. They are typically loaded with sugar, and are believed to be a major contributor to obesity. They can also contribute to type 2 diabetes, dental decay, nutrient deficiencies and even osteoporosis (possibly because people who drink lots of soft drinks don't drink enough milk). It's easier never to introduce your child to soft drinks than to try and wean her off them later. Cordials are in the same boat – there's simply no reason your toddler should be drinking them, and plenty of reasons she shouldn't.

- **Plenty of water –** toddlers need lots of water to keep them well hydrated and help prevent constipation. If your toddler has dry or pebbly poo, chances are she's not drinking enough water (she might also need more fibre in her diet). If you don't like the taste of plain water, make sure you don't deprive your toddler of the opportunity to develop a taste for it. Just think of all the sugar, salt and caffeine she will be spared over the course of her life if water is her drink of choice.

BREAKFAST TIME

• | • | • | • | • | • | • | • | • | • | • | • | • | • | • | • | • | • | • | • | • | • | • | • | • | • | • | • | • | • | •

It's something we've all heard many times before, but breakfast really is the most important meal of the day. Numerous studies have shown that children who eat breakfast have much better concentration and attention spans and perform better at school. They are also less likely to be overweight or at risk of heart disease. On the other hand, those who miss their morning meal are more likely to be irritable, tired, restless and easily distracted. They are also more likely to make poor food choices both for the rest of the day and over the long term, favouring high-fat and high-sugar options.

However, not all breakfasts are the same. There is no question that choosing a nutritious breakfast with a low glycaemic index (see page 128) is best for your child, as the slow release of energy will help keep her blood-sugar levels even and her tummy full for longer. What's more, if you can manage a balanced, healthy meal at breakfast time, when your toddler is not tired and cranky, it's less of a concern if lunch or dinner go badly, which is bound to happen from time to time. At least you've managed to include one good meal in her day.

BIRCHER MUESLI

SERVES 2 + TODDLER

• | • | • | • | • | • | • | • | • | • | • | • | • | •

This is a lovely summer alternative to porridge. If your toddler isn't a fan of the apple skin, you can peel the apple.

There is a limitless range of delicious toppings you can pop on your bircher muesli. Try finely chopped toasted almonds, chopped dried figs, or sesame seeds.

100 g (3½ oz/1 cup) rolled oats
2 tablespoons sultanas (golden raisins)
    or chopped dried apricots
185 ml (6 fl oz/¾ cup) milk
1 apple, grated with skin on
1 teaspoon ground cinnamon
90 g (3 oz/⅓ cup) plain yoghurt
2 tablespoons LSA or ground almonds
fruit of your choice, to serve

Combine the oats, sultanas and milk in a bowl. Cover with plastic wrap (cling film) and refrigerate for at least 1 hour (preferably overnight) to allow the milk to soak in.

Stir in the apple and cinnamon, divide the muesli among serving bowls and top with the yoghurt, LSA and fruit. For a young toddler, chop up the fruit and stir it through the muesli with the yoghurt.

Dairy-free alternative: If your toddler is on a dairy-free diet, you can replace the milk and yoghurt with 250 ml (8½ fl oz/1 cup) of rice milk, soy milk, apple juice or half apple juice and half water. You might also like to add a teaspoon of sesame seeds for an extra calcium boost.

COCONUT AND RASPBERRY PORRIDGE

SERVES 2 + TODDLER

• | • | • | • | • | • | • | • | • | • | • | • | • | •

The coconut milk adds a delicious creaminess to porridge. Coconut milk is high in saturated fat, but children do need some saturated fat for their development and coconut is a good, nutritious source. If you like, you can add less coconut milk and more water for a lighter porridge.

100 g (3½ oz/1 cup) rolled oats
160 ml (5½ fl oz/⅔ cup) coconut milk
1 tablespoon LSA, chia seeds or wheatgerm
1–2 teaspoons maple syrup (optional)
85 g (3 oz/⅔ cup) fresh or frozen raspberries
2 tablespoons plain yoghurt

Put the rolled oats in a saucepan with the coconut milk and 250 ml (8½ fl oz/1 cup) water. Cook over medium heat, stirring, for about 5 minutes or until the porridge has reached the desired consistency (you can add a little more liquid if required).

Stir through the LSA and maple syrup, then gently stir through the raspberries. If using frozen raspberries, leave the porridge on the heat for another minute or so to thaw the raspberries. Divide among serving bowls and top with the yoghurt.

APPLE AND CINNAMON PORRIDGE

SERVES 2 + TODDLER

• | • | • | • | • | • | • | • | • | • | • | • | • | •

Keep your toddler's morning porridge interesting by varying the grains and flavours. It's hard to beat freshly grated apple with cinnamon on a chilly winter morning.

50 g (2 oz/½ cup) rolled oats
50 g (2 oz/½ cup) millet
160 ml (5½ fl oz/⅔ cup) milk
1 apple, grated with skin on
1–2 teaspoons maple syrup, optional
1 tablespoon LSA, chia seeds, ground almonds or wheatgerm
¼ teaspoon ground cinnamon
milk, to serve

Put the rolled oats and millet in a saucepan with the milk and 250 ml (8½ fl oz/1 cup) water. Cook over medium heat, stirring, for 10–12 minutes. Stir through the grated apple and cook for a further 1 minute or until the porridge has reached the desired consistency (you can add a little more liquid if required).

Stir through the maple syrup, LSA and cinnamon. Divide among serving bowls and serve with a little milk.

QUINOA BUBBLES

SERVES 1 TODDLER

• | • | • | • | • | • | • | • | • | • | • | • | • | •

Quinoa is a grain-like seed that is an excellent source of protein and is also rich in iron, B vitamins, vitamin E and calcium. You can buy it from health food stores and some supermarkets. Puffed quinoa is a delicious and far healthier alternative to commercial puffed rice cereal.

Vary the quantity according to your toddler's appetite. You can also add another nutritional booster such as chia seeds, wheatgerm or linseed oil.

15 g (½ oz/½ cup) puffed quinoa
1 tablespoon LSA or ground almonds
fruit, plain yoghurt and milk, to serve

Place the puffed quinoa in a serving bowl and top with the LSA, fruit, yoghurt and milk.

> **Variation:** You might like to replace the puffed quinoa with other grains such as puffed millet, puffed rice, puffed amaranth or puffed kamut. Each has a different nutritional profile and the diversity is important for your toddler.

BLUEBERRY SAUCE

MAKES ABOUT 2 CUPS

• | • | • | • | • | • | • | • | • | • | • | • | • | •

This delicious, deep-blue sauce gives a stunning lift to pancakes, French toast, yoghurt, porridge, bircher muesli, rice pudding and just about anything else that takes your fancy.

310 g (11 oz/2 cups) frozen blueberries
juice of 2 oranges, about 250 ml
  (8½ fl oz/1 cup)
2 tablespoons maple syrup

Combine the blueberries, orange juice and maple syrup in a small saucepan over low–medium heat. Cook for about 10–15 minutes or until the blueberries are soft and the sauce has reduced and thickened a little.

Serve as is or purée the mixture in a blender. Set aside one serving and freeze the remainder in individual portions for later use.

* Suitable for freezing

> If your toddler is hooked on a commercial breakfast cereal, don't stress. You can significantly boost its nutritional profile by serving it with fresh fruit and mixing through a spoonful of LSA, ground almonds, wheatgerm, chia seeds, puffed quinoa, puffed amaranth, sesame seeds or plain yoghurt. You could also add a little dash of this blueberry sauce, maple syrup or some other sweet incentive until your toddler accepts these new tastes.

RASPBERRY PIKELETS

MAKES 15–20

• | • | • | • | • | • | • | • | • | • | • | • | • | • | •

These are healthier than traditional pikelets because they don't have added sugar and they include antioxidant-rich raspberries. Use blueberries If your toddler prefers them.

You can substitute half of the flour with wholemeal (whole-wheat) self-raising flour for an even healthier pikelet option.

150 g (5 oz/1 cup) self-raising flour
1 egg
250 ml (8½ fl oz/1 cup) milk or 125 ml
   (4 fl oz/½ cup) each of milk and buttermilk
40 g (1½ oz) butter, melted, plus extra,
   for cooking
60 g (2 oz/½ cup) fresh or frozen raspberries
maple syrup or jam (jelly), to serve

Sift the flour into a bowl. Make a well in the centre and add the egg, milk and melted butter. Start stirring the wet ingredients, gradually drawing in the dry ingredients until just combined. Do not overmix – the batter should be slightly lumpy. Gently stir through the berries.

Melt a little butter in a non-stick frying pan over medium heat. Drop tablespoons of the batter into the pan and cook for about 1 minute or until bubbles appear on the surface. Turn and cook the other side until golden. Repeat with the remaining mixture.

Serve the pikelets warm or cool, either plain or topped with a little maple syrup or jam.

* Suitable for freezing

RICOTTA PANCAKES

MAKES ABOUT 10

• | • | • | • | • | • | • | • | • | • | • | • | • | • | •

Your toddler will almost certainly want to take over the job of cooking these pancakes, spilling and dripping all over your bench and floor as he goes. Ah, the joys of parenthood.

If you don't eat them all, stack any leftovers between small squares of plastic wrap (cling film) and freeze in a snaplock bag for up to a month.

250 g (9 oz/1 cup) ricotta
1 tablespoon caster (superfine) sugar
1 egg
250 ml (8½ fl oz/1 cup) milk
150 g (5 oz/1 cup) self-raising flour
1 tablespoon olive oil
fresh fruit and maple syrup, to serve

Combine the ricotta, sugar and egg in a bowl. Stir in the milk and then the flour until just combined. Do not overmix – the batter should still be a little lumpy.

Heat half the oil in a large frying pan over medium heat. Pour 60 ml (2 fl oz/¼ cup) of the mixture into the pan for each pancake, leaving plenty of room between, then use the back of a spoon to spread to 10 cm (4 in) rounds. Cook for 1–2 minutes or until bubbles appear and the underside is golden. Flip and cook the other side.

Transfer the pancakes to a plate and cover them with a clean tea towel while you cook the remaining mixture. Top with fruit and a little drizzle of maple syrup to serve.

* Suitable for freezing

HOMEMADE BAKED BEANS

SERVES 2 + TODDLER

• ı • ı • ı • ı • ı • ı • ı • ı • ı • ı • ı

If you have an older toddler who has only ever seen baked beans come from a can, involve her in making this dish and you will be introducing her to the wonderful possibilities of the kitchen.

Legumes are fantastic foods – they're a great source of protein and also count towards one of your toddler's daily serve of vegetables.

400 g (14 oz) can cannellini beans, rinsed and drained
250 ml (8½ fl oz/1 cup) Vegetable pasta sauce (page 200)
1 tablespoon tomato sauce (ketchup)
toast, to serve

Place the beans, pasta sauce and tomato sauce in a medium saucepan and cook, stirring occasionally, over low–medium heat for about 5 minutes or until warmed through. Serve on toast.

MULTICOLOURED HASH BROWNS

MAKES ABOUT 12

• ı • ı • ı • ı • ı • ı • ı • ı • ı • ı • ı

The zucchini (courgette) and sweet potato in these hash browns provide your toddler with some of that essential vegetable variety that isn't always easy to achieve. They're lovely on their own, or with a poached egg or a little tomato sauce (ketchup).

If you cover the pan while the hash browns are cooking, the steam will help cook the vegetables. Keep the heat low and don't use too much oil, and there won't be much 'spitting'.

350 g (12 oz/2½ cups) mixed grated potato, sweet potato and zucchini (courgette)
3 tablespoons grated cheddar cheese
2 eggs
1 tablespoon plain (all-purpose) flour
2 teaspoons light olive oil

Use your hands to squeeze out as much moisture as you can from the grated vegetables. Put in a bowl with the cheese, eggs and flour and stir until well combined.

Heat ½ teaspoon of the oil in a frying pan over low heat and place large spoonfuls of the mixture into the pan. Lightly press and shape each one to form a hash brown. Cover and cook for 4–5 minutes or until golden underneath. Gently flip over and cook the other side, covered. Drain on paper towels. Repeat with the remaining oil and vegetable mixture.

NO-WASTE BREAKFAST PLATE
SERVES 2 + TODDLER

My husband hates food waste, and makes it his Sunday-morning mission to use whatever he can find in our fridge to make a fantastic family breakfast, while I read the papers.

The quantities in this recipe are vague – adjust them according to whatever you have on hand. Our son thinks it's fantastic and he has a great time squishing and tasting (and, I confess, sometimes spitting out) all the different fresh flavours.

handful of baby spinach or rocket (arugula), washed and drained
1 large tomato, diced
small handful of basil, shredded
small handful of pitted black olives
extra-virgin olive oil, for drizzling
handful of finely grated carrot or celeriac
handful of grated cheese
few spoonfuls of Homemade baked beans (see left)
few spoonfuls of Hummus (page 153)
½ avocado, sliced
3 eggs
buttered toast fingers, to serve

Place the spinach in a little mound on three serving plates. Top the spinach with the tomato, basil, olives and a light drizzle of olive oil. Place a small mound of the carrot, cheese, baked beans, hummus and avocado on each plate.

Lightly boil the eggs (cook for about 3–4 minutes after the water has reached boiling point). Slice off the tops and place an egg in an egg cup on each plate. Serve with toast fingers.

EGGS FU YUNG

SERVES 2 + TODDLER

• | • | • | • | • | • | • | • | • | • | • | • | • | • | • | •

This is a Chinese dish that traditionally includes chicken and prawns (shrimp). My mum used to make me this simplified version when I was a little girl. It makes a lovely breakfast or lunch with a splash of soy.

4 shiitake or button mushrooms
4 eggs
90 g (3 oz/1 cup) bean sprouts, chopped
1–2 spring onions (scallions), thinly sliced
1 teaspoon light olive oil
soy sauce or tamari, to serve

Finely slice the mushrooms, then roughly chop. Break the eggs into a large bowl and beat well. Add the chopped bean sprouts, spring onion and mushroom.

Heat the oil in a large non-stick frying pan over medium heat. Drop tablespoons of the egg mixture into the pan. Fry until lightly browned underneath, then turn and cook the other side until cooked through. Serve with a dash of soy sauce.

EGGS IN RAMEKINS

SERVES 2 + TODDLER

• | • | • | • | • | • | • | • | • | • | • | • | • | • | • | •

You can adjust the ingredients to use whatever tidbits take your toddler's fancy. For example, put some cooked mushroom in the ramekin, and top with an egg.

1 tomato, finely diced
1 slice ham or prosciutto (optional)
1 tablespoon finely chopped parsley or chives
2 spring onions (scallions), thinly sliced
3–5 eggs
½ teaspoon butter
toast fingers, to serve

Grease three ramekins and divide the tomato, ham, herbs and spring onion among them.

Place the ramekins in a saucepan or deep frying pan and add enough water to reach halfway up the sides of the dishes. Crack an egg (or two eggs, for an adult serve) into each ramekin and top with a dot of butter. Cover and cook over low heat for 5–7 minutes or until the eggs are set. Serve with toast fingers.

Runny eggs are not recommended for children under two years old (or pregnant women) because of the risk of salmonella infection. Although this risk still exists for older children, their more mature bodies are better able to cope in the event of infection. The best way to avoid the risk is to thoroughly cook egg whites and cook the yolks until they begin to thicken.

LUNCHBOXES AND PICNICS

• | • | • | • | • | • | • | • | • | • | • | • | • | • | • | • | • | • | • | • | • | • | • | • | • | • | • | • | • | • | • | •

When you're looking after an active toddler, lunch is one meal that is often eaten out of the house. If you're having a picnic at the park, or perhaps your toddler takes his own lunchbox to daycare, it's great to have a healthy, portable meal for him. The key is choosing meal options that are quick and easy (and not too messy), or that you can just pull from the freezer and thaw. While sandwiches are an obvious favourite, it's good to mix things up a bit to keep lunch interesting.

TODDLERS

ABC BUTTER SANDWICH

MAKES 1

• | • | • | • | • | • | • | • | • | • | • | • | • | • | • |

ABC butter? This is a peanut butter alternative made from almonds, brazil nuts and cashew nuts, and is available from many supermarkets and most health food stores. If your child is a peanut butter addict, try her on this instead. It's just as delicious and will provide her with some different tastes and nutrients.

If lunch is being eaten with other children, you'll need to first check whether any have a nut allergy.

2 slices wholemeal (whole-wheat) bread
1 tablespoon ABC butter
1 tablespoon finely grated carrot or
   ½ banana, thinly sliced

Spread one bread slice with the ABC butter and top with the carrot or banana. Place the other bread slice on top and cut into quarters or triangles.

OTHER NUTRITIOUS SANDWICH IDEAS

• Cream cheese, grated carrot and sultanas (golden raisins)

• Avocado, cheddar cheese and grated apple

• Finely diced boiled egg mixed with mayonnaise (don't use any mayonnaise with raw egg for a child under two years)

• Ricotta, avocado and finely diced dried figs

• Pesto (page 172) and cream cheese

• Tuna, mayonnaise and shredded lettuce

• Roasted sweet potato (soft enough to spread), cheddar cheese and avocado

• Nut butter (e.g. peanut or ABC), mashed banana and raisins

• Cannellini bean and tuna purée (see right)

You could also add some tahini (ground sesame seed paste) and a sprinkling of chia seeds to any of these sandwich combos for a nutritional boost and even greater variety.

If your toddler prefers crustless sandwiches, by all means remove the crusts. Crusts don't offer an additional nutritional benefit, although they can be good for chewing, which is important for gums.

HUMMUS

MAKES ABOUT 1¼ CUPS

Hummus is an absolute staple in our house – so much so, it was one of my son's first words. It's a great source of protein and it makes a wonderful toast topping and sandwich filling. I like to use it instead of butter.

Tahini is a paste made from ground-up sesame seeds, and is a good source of calcium for your toddler. It can also be spread on bread as an alternative to peanut butter.

400 g (14 oz) can no-added-salt chickpeas, rinsed and drained
2 tablespoons olive oil
2 tablespoons lemon juice
2 tablespoons plain yoghurt
½ garlic clove, roughly chopped
1 tablespoon tahini

Put all the ingredients in a food processor and blend until smooth.

> **Broccoli hummus:** Add 60 g (2 oz/1 cup) of steamed, chopped broccoli before blending for a greener, even more nutritious hummus. Try other cooked green vegetables, such as zucchini (courgette) or peas.

CANNELLINI BEAN AND TUNA PURÉE

MAKES ABOUT 2 CUPS

This purée is so easy to make and is seriously tasty spread on toast for an afternoon or morning snack. It also makes a great sandwich filling and a delicious dip. It's a wonderfully healthy source of protein for your toddler.

400 g (14 oz) can cannellini beans, rinsed and drained
180 g (6 oz) can tuna, drained
3 tablespoons olive oil
small handful of parsley or chives
2 tablespoons lemon juice
1 garlic clove
2 tablespoons plain yoghurt

Blend all the ingredients in a food processor until well combined and smooth.

> I try to use tuna sparingly in my household as it generally comes from unsustainable sources and I really would prefer it if there are still some fish in the ocean by the time my son is an adult. Some brands are more sustainable than others – check out Greenpeace's website for more information.

TOMATO AND ZUCCHINI BAKE

MAKES 1 LOAF

Although my son can spit out zucchini (courgettes) faster than the speed of light, he will happily eat them in this dead-simple, nutritious dish. Best of all, you can freeze it – slice, wrap in plastic wrap (cling film) and store in an airtight container for up to a month.

You might like to replace half the flour with wholemeal (whole-wheat) self-raising flour for an even more wholesome loaf.

4 zucchini (courgettes), coarsely grated
1 onion, finely chopped
150 g (5 oz/1 cup) self-raising flour
5 eggs, lightly beaten
90 g (3 oz/¾ cup) grated cheddar cheese
3 tablespoons grated parmesan
3 tablespoons light olive oil
6–8 cherry tomatoes, halved

Preheat the oven to 200°C (400°F). Grease a 14 x 21 cm loaf tin. Line the base and two long sides with baking paper, leaving the ends overhanging to make it easier to remove the loaf from the tin.

Squeeze the grated zucchini with your hands to remove the excess moisture. Combine in a bowl with the onion, flour, eggs, cheeses and oil.

Spoon the mixture into the prepared tin and top with the tomato, cut side up. Bake for 1 hour or until a skewer inserted into the centre comes out clean. Leave in the tin to cool slightly, then lift out and cut into thick slices.

* Suitable for freezing

SAUSAGE ROLLS

MAKES 24 MINI ROLLS

Much better than store-bought ones, you know that nothing artificial has gone into your lovely homemade sausage rolls. I use parsley and thyme because I have them growing in my herb garden, but you can substitute with the herbs you have handy. Even a little mint, oregano and basil works well.

You can freeze these sausage rolls before or after they are cooked. If you freeze them before cooking, there is no need to defrost them – just bake them for an extra 10 or 15 minutes.

450 g (1 lb) minced (ground) beef

155 g (5 oz/1 cup) finely grated carrot

70 g (2½ oz/½ cup) finely grated zucchini (courgette)

2 spring onions (scallions), halved lengthways and thinly sliced

2 tablespoons finely chopped flat-leaf parsley

1 teaspoon thyme leaves

2 tablespoons tomato sauce (ketchup)

2 x 24 cm (9½ in) squares frozen puff pastry, thawed

1 egg, lightly beaten

2 tablespoons sesame seeds

Preheat the oven to 200°C (400°F). Line a baking tray with baking paper.

Place the minced beef in a large bowl. Using your hands, lightly squeeze the grated carrot and zucchini to remove some of the excess moisture. Add to the bowl, along with the spring onion, herbs and tomato sauce and mix until well combined.

Cut each pastry sheet in half and place on a board. Place a quarter of the beef mixture along the centre of each pastry sheet. Lightly brush the pastry edges with water and fold over the filling, pressing the edges together to seal. Turn the pastry over so the seam is underneath.

Brush each roll with beaten egg and sprinkle with the sesame seeds. Cut each roll into six pieces and place on the prepared tray. Bake for about 25 minutes or until the pastry is golden.

* Suitable for freezing

BEEF AND ZUCCHINI MEATBALLS

MAKES ABOUT 40

Thanks to the bread and zucchini (courgette) in this recipe, these meatballs are light, tender and more delicious than any other I've tried. I like to use wholemeal (whole-wheat) bread, but white will also do the trick if that's what you have on hand.

You can cover the frying pan with a lid after the meatballs have browned, as the steam will help them cook through. However, don't use the lid for the whole cooking time as they will stew, rather than brown.

3 tablespoons light olive oil
1 brown onion, finely diced
3 slices wholemeal (whole-wheat) bread, crusts removed, roughly chopped
3 tablespoons milk
500 g (1 lb 2 oz) minced (ground) beef
135 g (5 oz/1 cup) finely grated zucchini (courgette)
¼ teaspoon ground paprika

Heat 1 tablespoon of the oil in a frying pan over medium heat and cook the onion until soft. Set aside to cool.

Put the bread and milk in a large bowl and leave to stand for 1 minute to allow the milk to soak in. Add the cooked onion, beef, zucchini and paprika and mix with your hands until the bread is broken up and the mixture is well combined. Roll into 3–4 cm (1–1.5 in) balls.

Heat the remaining oil in a frying pan over medium heat. Cook the meatballs in batches until they are golden and cooked through.

* Suitable for freezing

> **Spaghetti and meatballs:** These meatballs are also lovely for dinner. Just stir them through some Vegetable pasta sauce (page 200) or a tomato pasta sauce and serve with spaghetti and a little grated cheese on top.

ASIAN CHICKEN BITES

MAKES ABOUT 25

These are a perfect toddler food – easy to eat, really tasty and a good way to introduce your child to some new flavours, such as ginger and coriander (cilantro). You might like to toss some through a mixed green salad for yourself.

350 g chicken breast, roughly chopped
½ teaspoon grated ginger
3 tablespoons chopped coriander (cilantro) leaves (optional)
2 spring onions (scallions), roughly chopped
5 green beans, roughly chopped
1 teaspoon soy sauce or tamari
1 egg
2 tablespoons light olive oil

Place the chicken breast, ginger, coriander, spring onions, beans and soy sauce in the bowl of a food processor and process until almost smooth. Add the egg and process until combined.

Heat the oil in a large frying pan over medium heat. Drop heaped teaspoons of the chicken mixture into the hot pan and cook for 1–2 minutes each side or until golden and cooked through. Drain on paper towels. Serve warm or cool.

* Suitable for freezing

I know a number of children who don't like the taste of coriander (cilantro). As with any food, I think it's simply a matter of developing a taste for it. My son has had coriander since soon after starting solids and he happily eats it now. It may take a few tastes, but your child will no doubt accept it before too long.

'Roasted capsicum makes a perfect finger food. Drizzle with olive oil and roast in a 220°C (430°F) oven until the skin starts to brown and bubble. Remove the skin with your fingers and cut into strips.'

MINI SPANISH OMELETTE

SERVES 1 + TODDLER

• ı •

This potato omelette can be served warm or cold cut into fingers. It also makes a great dinner on those days when you haven't had a chance to do the shopping and your fridge is down to the bare essentials. If you don't have capsicum (pepper), you can use broccoli or whatever vegetables you have on hand.

An alternative to turning the omelette onto a plate and returning it to the pan is to finish it under a grill (broiler). Wrap the handle of your frying pan in foil to prevent it from burning.

Heat the oil in a 20 cm (8 in) non-stick frying pan over low–medium heat. Cook the potato, capsicum, onion and garlic, covered, for about 10 minutes or until very tender, stirring occasionally.

Beat the eggs with the parmesan and chives. Pour the egg mixture evenly into the pan and cook, covered, for about 8 minutes or until the omelette is just set. Run a spatula around the edge of the pan, then carefully turn it out onto a plate and slide it back into the pan with the cooked side facing up. Cook for a couple of minutes until the bottom side is golden. Slide onto a plate, allow to cool a little, then cut into wedges or fingers.

1 teaspoon light olive oil

80 g (3 oz/¾ cup) diced potato

80 g (3 oz/½ cup) diced red capsicum (pepper)

80 g (3 oz/½ cup) finely diced onion or thinly sliced leek

1 garlic clove, crushed or finely diced

3–4 eggs

1 tablespoon grated parmesan

2 teaspoons finely snipped chives

BANANA, HAZELNUT AND HONEY BREAD

MAKES 1 LOAF

I simply adore this banana bread. It's easy to make and totally delicious, and you'll feel like a domestic goddess for having made your very own instead of picking it up from your local café.

You can cut the loaf into thick slices, wrap them in plastic wrap (cling film) and freeze. Simply defrost and heat in the toaster or microwave when you're ready to eat.

225 g (8 oz/1½ cups) self-raising flour
55 g (2 oz/½ cup) ground hazelnuts
3 tablespoons soft brown sugar
½ teaspoon ground cinnamon
240 g (8½ oz/1 cup) mashed banana
   (about 2 bananas)
3 tablespoons milk
125 ml (4 fl oz/½ cup) hazelnut oil or
   light olive oil
2 eggs, lightly beaten
2 tablespoons honey
120 g (4 oz/¾ cup) pitted, chopped dates
2 tablespoons chopped hazelnuts (optional)

Preheat the oven to 170°C (340°F). Grease a 25 cm (10 in) loaf (bar) tin. Line the base and two long sides with baking paper, leaving the ends overhanging to make it easier to remove the loaf from the tin.

Sift the flour into a bowl and add the ground hazelnuts, sugar and cinnamon. Make a well in the centre and add the remaining ingredients, stirring until the mixture is just combined – do not overmix.

Pour the mixture into the prepared tin and bake for about 1 hour or until a skewer inserted into the centre comes out clean. Leave in the tin for 5 minutes, then lift out and transfer to a wire rack to cool.

* Suitable for freezing

> **Variations:** Replace the dates with prunes or sultanas (golden raisins). You don't need to add the chopped hazelnuts, but they do add a lovely crunch. If you prefer, you can replace them with chopped walnuts or pepitas (pumpkin seeds).

APPLE, BANANA AND MACADAMIA NUT COOKIES

MAKES ABOUT 32

• •

With egg allergies unfortunately on the rise, these delicious egg-free cookies are just the thing when you're having a playdate with other children.

1 large banana, mashed

125 g (4 oz) butter, softened and diced

60 g (2 oz/⅓ cup) soft brown sugar

2 tablespoons milk

75 g (2½ oz/½ cup) self-raising flour

110 g (4 oz/¾ cup) wholemeal (whole-wheat) self-raising flour

100 g (3½ oz/1 cup) rolled oats

½ teaspoon ground cinnamon

80 g (3 oz/½ cup) macadamia nuts, roughly chopped

1 apple, grated with skin on

Preheat the oven to 180°C (350°F). Grease two baking trays or line with baking paper. Mix the mashed banana with the butter, brown sugar and milk.

In a separate bowl, sift the flours, returning any sifted husks from the wholemeal flour, then stir in the oats, cinnamon, macadamia nuts and apple. Add the banana mixture and stir until just combined.

Drop spoonfuls of the mixture onto the prepared trays and bake for 15 minutes or until golden brown.

* Suitable for freezing

FRUITY MUESLI SQUARES

MAKES 24

These muesli squares are packed full of goodness and are much healthier than store-bought ones. The high seed content – sesame, pepita (pumpkin) and sunflower – is a wonderful way of ensuring your toddler is getting a nice serve of essential fats, selenium, vitamin E, calcium and zinc. The message from leading nutritionists is to include plenty of seeds in your child's diet for good brain function.

Bear in mind that these are quite sweet, so offer one as a treat during high-activity times.

125 g (4 oz) butter
60 g (2 oz/⅓ cup) soft brown sugar
2 tablespoons honey
150 g (5 oz/1½ cups) rolled oats
75 g (2½ oz/½ cup) self-raising flour
60 g (2 oz/½ cup) sultanas (golden raisins)
75 g (2½ oz/½ cup) chopped dried apricots
3 tablespoons sesame seeds
3 tablespoons sunflower seeds
3 tablespoons chopped pepitas (pumpkin seeds) (or you can use chopped walnuts)

Preheat the oven to 180°C (350°F) and grease a shallow 18 x 25 cm (7 x 10 in) cake tin. Line the base and two long sides with baking paper, leaving the ends overhanging to make it easier to remove from the tin.

Stir the butter, sugar and honey in a saucepan over low–medium heat until the butter has melted and the sugar has dissolved.

Combine the remaining ingredients in a large bowl. Stir through the butter mixture until well combined.

Press the mixture firmly into the tin with a metal spoon and bake for about 20 minutes or until golden. Cool completely in the tin before lifting out and cutting into 24 squares with a heavy sharp knife.

* Suitable for freezing

When buying dried apricots, I try to choose a brand with no added sulphur dioxide (organic brands are generally sulphur-free). Sulphur dioxide (220) is a preservative that has been associated with a range of food intolerance symptoms, including headaches and rashes, and which particularly affects asthma sufferers.

APRICOT AND COCONUT BALLS

MAKES ABOUT 28

These apricot balls are so good for so many reasons – they're really easy to make, they're extremely nutritious, kids love them (and you will too), they look gorgeous, and they store well in the fridge. Make them on the weekend and your family can enjoy them in their lunchboxes all of the following week.

200 g (7 oz) dried apricots
1 tablespoon fresh orange juice
2 tablespoons boiling water
65 g (2 oz/¾ cup) desiccated (shredded) coconut
50 g (2 oz/½ cup) ground almonds
3 tablespoons wheatgerm

Place the apricots in the small bowl of a food processor and blend until finely chopped. Add the orange juice and boiling water and leave to soak in for 1 minute.

Add 45 g (1½ oz/½ cup) of the coconut, the ground almonds and wheatgerm, and blend until the mixture forms a smooth paste.

Using your hands, roll the mixture into small balls and then roll in the remaining coconut. Store in an airtight container in the fridge for up to a week.

Variation: To increase your toddler's dietary variety, you might like to replace half of the apricots with dried figs. Like apricots, figs are a good source of iron.

APPLE CINNAMON TURNOVERS

MAKES 8

Filled with delicious apple and raisins, these are perfect for a toddler party. Cut them in half to make them easy for little hands to hold and to reveal the yummy filling inside.

Both shortcrust and puff pastry work beautifully – puff pastry will produce flaky turnovers.

2 large green apples, peeled, cored and cut into 1 cm (½ in) cubes

2 tablespoons raisins or sultanas (golden raisins)

½ teaspoon ground cinnamon

1 tablespoon soft brown sugar

2 x 24 cm (9½ in) squares frozen shortcrust or puff pastry

1 egg, lightly beaten

Preheat the oven to 200°C (400°F). Line two baking trays with baking paper.

Put the apple in a saucepan with 3 tablespoons water and cook over medium heat for about 8–10 minutes or until tender. Drain the apple in a sieve to remove any excess moisture.

Mix the apple, raisins, cinnamon and sugar in a bowl until well combined.

Cut each pastry sheet into quarters. Using a sharp knife, round off the corners of each square to make a circle. Divide the apple mixture among the centres of the circles. Fold the pastry over and, using your fingers, roll the edges to seal. Place on the prepared trays and brush with the egg. Bake for about 18 minutes or until golden.

* Suitable for freezing

IN THE KITCHEN WITH YOUR TODDLER

Put on your apron and have the mop and dustpan ready – it's time to bring your toddler into the kitchen. I'm sure that, like me, you generally prefer to keep your child as far away from your cooking as possible. My son's capacity for making a mess of my kitchen is truly mind-boggling. But when I think of the extraordinary patience of my own parents and all the benefits that my son's involvement in the kitchen will bring (not least that he might make a meal for me some day!), I'm willing to live with the chaos. As you work through these recipes, remember that it's more about the process than the end result. Be prepared for a fair bit of mayhem, and hopefully a whole lot of fun.

FRUIT SMOOTHIE

SERVES 2–3

Most toddlers will eat some fruit without too much fuss. If yours isn't one of them, a smoothie might be the answer. Just call it a milkshake and she'll never know how much goodness she's drinking. You can also pour the smoothie into iceblock moulds and freeze for delicious, healthy iceblocks.

The tofu offers a boost of protein, as well as some iron, calcium, vitamin E and omega-3 fats.

about 1 cup chopped fruit (choose from banana, strawberry, papaya, mango or mixed berries)
3 tablespoons plain yoghurt
250 ml (8½ fl oz/1 cup) milk, rice milk or soy milk
1 tablespoon honey
1 tablespoon wheatgerm
1 teaspoon tahini
2 cm (¾ in) slice silken tofu (optional)
4 ice cubes

Place all the ingredients in a blender and process until smooth and frothy.

Papaya is a wonderful 'superfruit' to add to a smoothie. It is a good source of vitamins A, C and E, as well as calcium, iron, phosphorus and potassium. Many of these nutrients are found in green vegetables, so if your toddler is not so good with her greens, try introducing more papaya into her diet.

WHOLEMEAL PESTO PIKELETS

MAKES 15–20

• • • • • • • • • • • • • • • • • • • •

These are easy enough to involve an older toddler in the cooking. Just make sure you use a really big bowl and let him carefully stir as you add the ingredients.

150 g (5 oz/1 cup) wholemeal (whole-wheat) self-raising flour
40 g (1½ oz/⅓ cup) grated cheddar cheese
1 egg
250 ml (8½ fl oz/1 cup) milk or 125 ml (4 fl oz/½ cup) each of milk and buttermilk
40 g (1½ oz) butter, melted, plus extra, for cooking
1 tablespoon pesto (see right)
1 tablespoon chia seeds (optional)

Combine the flour and cheese in a large bowl. Make a well in the centre and add the egg, milk and melted butter. Start stirring the wet ingredients, gradually drawing in the dry ingredients until just combined. Do not overmix – the batter should be slightly lumpy. Gently stir through the pesto and chia seeds.

Melt a little butter in a non-stick frying pan over medium heat. Drop tablespoons of the batter into the pan and cook for 1 minute or until bubbles appear on the surface. Turn and cook the other side until golden. Serve the pikelets warm or cool.

PESTO

MAKES ABOUT 1 CUP

• • • • • • • • • • • • • • • • • • • •

Homemade pesto is just about the most nutritionally dense food I can imagine. I make mine with different fresh greens from my vegetable garden, along with plenty of mixed nuts and seeds, garlic, parmesan and good-quality olive oil. It will happily keep in the fridge for a week with a drizzle of olive oil over the surface.

You can include pesto in just about any meal. I make my son ricotta or cream cheese sandwiches mixed with pesto and he adores them. You can also stir it through hot or cold pasta, or spoon it onto a baked potato or over grilled meats.

75 g (2½ oz/1½ cups) firmly packed basil leaves, or use a mixture of basil, parsley, baby spinach and raw broccoli
50 g (2 oz/⅓ cup) pine nuts, walnuts, cashew nuts or almonds, or use a mixture and throw in some pepitas (pumpkin seeds)
35 g (1 oz/⅓ cup) grated parmesan
½ garlic clove, chopped
3–4 tablespoons good-quality olive oil

In the small bowl of a food processor, blend the herbs, nuts, cheese and garlic until almost smooth, occasionally scraping down the side. Add the oil in a slow, thin stream and blend until smooth.

TUNA AND CARROT PINWHEELS

MAKES 40

• •

Toddlers love these sandwiches because they get to use a rolling pin and do some spreading with a spatula. Of course, they make a huge mess, but at least it's just bread that they're mangling – not a delicate dough that risks being ruined with overhandling.

These pinwheels are also perfect party food because they can be made ahead, and sliced just as the guests arrive.

95 g (3 oz) can tuna, drained
125 g (4 oz) spreadable cream cheese
1 spring onion (scallion), thinly sliced
2 tablespoons finely grated carrot
8 thin slices wholemeal (whole-wheat) bread,
  crusts removed
finely snipped herbs, to serve

Mix the tuna, cream cheese, spring onion and grated carrot in a bowl until well combined, breaking up any chunks of tuna.

Place the bread on a board and flatten each slice with a rolling pin until very thin. Top each slice with a slightly heaped tablespoon of the tuna mixture. Spread to the edges and roll up tightly.

Wrap the rolled bread slices tightly with plastic wrap (cling film), then twist the ends to secure and refrigerate until required.

Slice each roll into four or five pieces, about 2 cm (¾ in) wide. Arrange on a plate and garnish with some finely snipped herbs.

CHEESY VEGETABLE MUFFINS

MAKES 16

● ● ● ● ● ● ● ● ● ● ● ● ● ● ● ● ●

These muffins are another tasty way of ensuring your toddler is getting plenty of vegetables. I like to cook them when my friends come to visit, because they love them as much as their toddlers do.

For a pretty finishing touch, top each muffin with a halved cherry tomato before baking.

375 g (13 oz/2½ cups) self-raising flour
310 ml (10½ fl oz/1¼ cups) milk
80 ml (3 fl oz/⅓ cup) light olive oil
1 egg, lightly beaten
70 g (2½ oz/½ cup) grated zucchini
  (courgette) or broccoli
80 g (3 oz/½ cup) grated carrot
125 g (4 oz/1 cup) grated cheddar cheese
½ bunch chives, finely snipped

Preheat the oven to 190°C (375°F). Line 16 x 80 ml (3 fl oz/⅓ cup) muffin holes with silicone or paper cases. Sift the flour into a large bowl, then stir through the remaining ingredients until just combined – do not overmix.

Spoon the batter into the muffin cases and bake for 25 minutes, or until a skewer inserted into the centre comes out clean. Transfer to a wire rack to cool. Serve warm or at room temperature.

* Suitable for freezing

HOMEMADE PASTA DOUGH

MAKES 300 G (10½ OZ) PASTA (SERVES 4)

● ● ● ● ● ● ● ● ● ● ● ● ● ● ● ● ●

This basic pasta dough can be used to make your own ravioli (page 177) or whichever pasta is your toddler's favourite – spaghetti, pappardelle, tortellini – the options are almost endless.

200 g (7 oz/1⅓ cups) plain (all-purpose) flour
½ teaspoon salt
2 large eggs

Place the flour and salt in a food processor. With the motor running, add the eggs one at a time. Continue processing for about 2 minutes or until the dough is elastic and firm. If the dough hasn't combined, add 1–2 tablespoons water, keeping the motor running until the correct texture is achieved. If it is a little wet, simply use more flour when kneading.

Turn the dough out on to a floured surface. Knead lightly and wrap in plastic wrap (cling film). Leave to rest for 30 minutes before rolling.

Set the rollers of a pasta machine at the maximum opening. Cut the dough in half. Flatten one of the pieces and run it through the machine. Fold this sheet in thirds, give it a quarter turn and run it through the machine again. Repeat this three more times, until the dough feels smooth and elastic and has a satiny glow. Repeat with the other half of the dough.

Reduce the opening of the machine one notch and run the strips through the machine again, one at a time. Lay the sheets on a cloth as they are done.

RICOTTA AND SPINACH RAVIOLI
SERVES 4

· ·

When I was a kid I thought my parents were crazy to make their own pasta when you could buy so many different types at the shops. Nevertheless, I happily joined in, taking turns with my sister to carefully pull the dough through our old pasta machine. I can now see that those hours spent together were precious lessons in self-sufficiency, doing things properly and working together as a family.

150 g (5 oz) baby spinach leaves
300 g (10½ oz) ricotta
grated rind of 1 lemon
35 g (1 oz/⅓ cup) grated parmesan
1 quantity Homemade pasta dough (page 175)
1 egg, lightly beaten
olive oil and parmesan shavings, to serve
  (optional)

Tomato sauce
2 tablespoons olive oil
1 small onion, diced
1 garlic clove, sliced
400 g (14 oz) can no-added-salt peeled
  chopped tomatoes

First make the filling. Wash and lightly drain the spinach. Place in a saucepan with a tight-fitting lid and cook over medium heat for 4–5 minutes or until wilted and just tender. Drain thoroughly and cool, then squeeze out the excess water and chop finely.

Combine the spinach in a bowl with the ricotta, lemon rind and grated parmesan. Set aside.

To make the tomato sauce, heat the oil in a saucepan over medium heat and cook the onion and garlic for 3–5 minutes or until the onion is soft but not brown. Add the chopped tomatoes and simmer over low heat for 20 minutes. Blend the sauce in a food processor or with a stick blender until smooth.

Roll the pasta as thinly as possible into sheets about 8 cm (3 in) wide. Cover with a damp tea towel.

Spoon 1 tablespoon of the ricotta mixture in mounds along half of the pasta sheets, about 8 cm (3 in) apart. Brush the egg along the edges of the pasta sheets and between each spoonful of mixture. Lay one of each of the remaining pasta sheets over each of the filled sheets.

Using your fingers, seal the edges, pushing out the air around the filling. Use a sharp knife to trim the edges and cut the ravioli into squares. Pinch the edges to make sure they're sealed.

Bring a large saucepan of water to the boil. Cook the ravioli in two or three batches over high heat for about 6 minutes or until cooked through. Remove the ravioli with a slotted spoon and drain thoroughly.

Serve the ravioli over the tomato sauce, drizzle with the oil and sprinkle with parmesan shavings.

PROSCIUTTO AND MUSHROOM PIZZA

MAKES 6 SMALL PIZZAS

· | · | · | · | · | · | · | · | · | · | · | · | · | · | · | · | · | · | · | · | · | · | · | · | · | · | · | · | · | · | · | · | · |

There are few cooking experiences that are as much fun as making your own pizza. It's a wonderful way to introduce your child to the simple pleasure of making a favourite meal from scratch.

300 g (10½ oz/2 cups) plain
   (all-purpose) flour
1 teaspoon salt
1 teaspoon sugar
7 g (¼ oz) sachet dried yeast
3 tablespoons olive oil
125 ml (4 fl oz/½ cup) tomato passata
   (puréed tomatoes)
1–2 garlic cloves, finely chopped
8 button mushrooms, thinly sliced
extra-virgin olive oil, to drizzle
100 g (3½ oz) prosciutto or ham, torn
8 bocconcini, torn into small pieces
small handful of basil leaves, chopped

Sift the flour and salt into a large bowl and stir in the sugar and yeast. Make a well in the centre and add the oil and 200 ml (7 fl oz) lukewarm water. Mix to a dough, then turn out onto a well-floured surface and knead for 4–5 minutes or until smooth. Put the dough in a greased bowl, cover with a tea towel and allow to rise in a warm place for about 1 hour or until doubled in size.

Preheat the oven to 220°C (430°F). Lightly flour two or three baking trays. Turn the dough out onto a floured surface and divide into six equal balls. Roll each ball into an oval shape to make thin pizza bases. Carefully transfer to the prepared trays.

Combine the tomato passata and garlic and spread over the bases, leaving a 1 cm (½ in) border around the edge. Scatter the mushrooms over the pizzas, drizzle with a little olive oil and bake for 7–10 minutes. Remove from the oven, top with the prosciutto and bocconcini, and bake for a further 5–10 minutes or until the bases are crisp and the cheese has melted. Sprinkle with the basil leaves and serve immediately.

Pizza is a great way to get kids to eat foods they usually might not touch, particularly if they've decorated it themselves. Try topping pizza with thinly sliced zucchini (courgette), capsicum (pepper), rocket (arugula) or any other vegetables you have on hand.

CHOC-BANANA AND STRAWBERRY POPS

MAKES 24

• I • I • I • I • I • I • I • I • I • I • I • I • I • I • I • I • I • I • I • I • I • I • I • I •

Although chocolate shouldn't feature regularly on your toddler's menu, making these as a special treat is bound to be the highlight of her day. They're a good one for toddlers who aren't keen on fruit. A dip of chocolate is sure to change her mind!

The strawberries will be too hard if they are fully frozen. They are best after just a couple of hours in the freezer. Alternatively, place them in the fridge to set, instead of the freezer.

150 g (5 oz) milk or dark chocolate
3 bananas
12 large strawberries

Line a baking tray with baking paper. Using scissors, cut 12 wooden ice cream sticks in half.

Break the chocolate into small, even pieces and place in a heatproof bowl. Fill a small saucepan one-third full with water. Bring to the boil, then reduce the heat to low. Put the chocolate bowl on top of the saucepan (it shouldn't be touching the water). Stir until melted and smooth (use a metal or silicone spoon – a wooden spoon can contain too many impurities for chocolate).

Meanwhile, peel the bananas and cut each into four pieces. Wash, dry and hull the strawberries. Push a half stick into each piece of fruit.

Dip the fruit pieces about halfway into the chocolate. Place on the prepared tray. Freeze for about 2 hours or until set. Serve partially frozen.

CARROT CUPCAKES WITH LEMON CREAM CHEESE ICING

MAKES 10

• ı •

These lovely cupcakes are very moist and tasty, and much more nutritious than regular cupcakes. I cooked them for my mother, an ex-Cordon Bleu pastry chef, and she thought they were perfect. Make a double quantity if you're catering for a crowd.

2 eggs, lightly beaten
3 tablespoons milk
95 g (3 oz/½ cup) soft brown sugar
125 ml (4 fl oz/½ cup) light olive oil
155 g (5 oz/1 cup) grated carrot
55 g (2 oz/½ cup) ground almonds
150 g (5 oz/1 cup) self-raising flour
½ teaspoon ground cinnamon

Lemon cream cheese icing (frosting)
150 g (5 oz) block cream cheese, softened
40 g (1½ oz/⅓ cup) icing (confectioners')
   sugar, sifted
3 teaspoons lemon juice

Preheat the oven to 180°C (350°F). Line 10 x 80 ml (3 fl oz/⅓-cup) muffin holes with paper or silicone cases.

Whisk together the eggs, milk, sugar and oil. Stir in the carrot and almonds. Sift in the flour and cinnamon, and stir until just combined.

Divide the mixture among the cupcake cases and bake for about 20 minutes or until a skewer inserted into the centre comes out clean. Leave in the tin for 5 minutes, then transfer to a wire rack to cool.

To make the icing, beat the cream cheese, icing sugar and lemon juice together until well combined and smooth. Add a little more lemon juice if you like a stronger lemon flavour.

Spread the icing over the top of the cooled cupcakes.

COCONUT AND PEACH ICEBLOCKS

MAKES 6

If you're fed up with craft projects, why not take your ice cream sticks to the kitchen and make some iceblocks with your toddler? You can use just about any fruit you like – bananas and berries work well.

250 g (9 oz/1 cup) plain yoghurt
125 ml (4 fl oz/½ cup) coconut milk
  or coconut cream
2 tablespoons maple syrup
200 g (7 oz/1 cup) drained canned
  peach slices

Put all the ingredients in a blender and process until smooth. Divide the mixture among six iceblock moulds. Place in the freezer for 1 hour or until partially frozen.

Using scissors, trim six wooden ice cream sticks so they're a suitable length for your moulds. Remove the moulds from the freezer and push an ice cream stick into each one. Return to the freezer for 3–4 hours or until well set.

Turn the iceblocks out of the moulds and serve.

> **Variation:** If fresh peaches are in season, use them instead of the canned peaches. You'll need to peel them and pop them in the blender. Use enough peaches to make about 250 ml (8½ fl oz/1 cup) of peach purée.

7

FAMILY MEALS

FAMILY MEALS FOR ALL AGES

If you're a parent, chances are your life is hectic and every spare minute is precious. It is completely understandable that you wouldn't want to spend hours shopping and cooking special food for your baby or toddler separate from the rest of the family.

There's a lot to be said for encouraging your child to eat exactly the same meal as you from as early as possible. Not only does it spare you from the nuisance of having to prepare two dinners every night, it's also most likely to result in your child having a varied diet and being willing to try different foods.

Once your baby is established on solids, you can start to be quite adventurous with his meals and simply prepare him the same food that the rest of the family is eating, puréeing and mashing it in the early months until he's old enough to manage finger foods. You just need to take care not to add any salt or other ingredients on the list of foods and drinks to avoid (see page 42). Of course, not every family meal will be suitable for a young baby – leafy salads or hot curries might be no good, for example – but a simple dish of fish or chicken with vegetables is perfect.

All the meals in this chapter are suitable from six months onwards and I've provided suggestions for how you can tweak them for your baby and toddler. The desserts are definitely on the healthier side of the dessert spectrum, but they do have some added sugar so you might prefer to give your baby only a small taste or save them until after his first birthday.

As difficult as it can be when you're a busy family and everyone has different schedules, it's worthwhile trying to include your child at the dinner table as often as you can. Mealtimes are an important social occasion and you'll be teaching him from a young age about how to be a good dining companion. What's more, studies have shown enormous health, educational and social benefits for older children who are in the habit of sitting down for meals with the rest of the family (see page 46).

Above all, family meals are a precious time to step away from the computer, put down the phone, turn off the television and talk to one another. I can't think of a more important way of spending my time.

SERVING SIZES

Because babies and toddlers eat such widely varying amounts, the serving sizes given in this chapter are for adults. In the case of baby purées, it's quite useful to have an adult-sized serving for your baby, because you can set aside one portion and then freeze the remainder in separate portions for later meals.

In the case of your toddler, you may like to adjust the quantities according to your toddler's usual appetite. However, I find it handy to have leftovers from last night's meal in the fridge – it saves having to make something from scratch for lunch.

SEASONINGS

As a general rule, these recipes don't include salt and pepper. Added salt is really bad news for children – their less mature kidneys can't cope and too much will give them a taste preference for salty foods (see page 131). Nutritionally, pepper is great, but many children find it too hot. However, after setting aside your child's serving, by all means season your food as you normally would (although most adults can benefit from a lower salt diet too).

CHICKEN STOCK

MAKES 1.5 LITRES (51 FL OZ/6 CUPS)

• | • | • | • | •| • | • | • | • | • | • | • | • | • | • | • | •

I have never found a commercial stock that tastes anything like a homemade one. Once you get in the habit of making your own stock, you'll never want to go back.

If you have a pressure cooker, use that instead of the stovetop – it produces an even richer, deeper flavour in about half the time.

1 kg (2 lb 3 oz) chicken carcass or bones
1 onion, diced
1 carrot, diced
2 celery stalks, diced
1 teaspoon salt
few black peppercorns
1 bay leaf
few sprigs parsley and thyme

Place all the ingredients in a large saucepan with 2 litres (68 fl oz/8 cups) water. Bring to the boil, skim the surface, then reduce the heat to low and simmer, uncovered, for 2 hours.

Strain the stock through a fine sieve, allow to cool, then refrigerate or freeze until needed.

* Suitable for freezing

VEGETABLE STOCK

MAKES 1.75 LITRES (59 FL OZ/7 CUPS)

• | • | • | • | • | • | • | • | • | • | • | • | • | • | • | • | •

Don't even think about throwing out those past-their-prime vegetables at the bottom of your crisper. They make the perfect base for a lovely flavoursome vegetable stock that will bring your soups and risottos to life.

1 onion, diced
1 carrot, diced
1 leek, diced
3 celery stalks, diced
few slices fresh ginger
1 teaspoon salt
few black peppercorns
1 bay leaf
few sprigs parsley and thyme

Place all the ingredients in a large saucepan with 2 litres (68 fl oz/8 cups) water. Bring to the boil, skim the surface, then reduce the heat to low and simmer, uncovered, for 1 hour.

Strain the stock through a fine sieve, allow to cool, then refrigerate or freeze until needed.

* Suitable for freezing

FAVOURITE PUMPKIN SOUP

SERVES 4–6

• | • | • | • | • | • | • | • | • | • | • | • | • | • | • | • | • | • | • | • | • | • | • | • | • | • | • | • | • | •

This was one of my favourites as a child and my son loves it too. Use homemade chicken stock (see left) if you have it. If you're buying stock, go for a salt-reduced one. This recipe makes enough for the whole family, or you can freeze any leftovers for another meal.

30 g (1 oz) butter

1 onion, diced

2 garlic cloves, diced

2 bacon rashers, diced (optional)

½ teaspoon ground nutmeg

1 kg (2 lb 3 oz) pumpkin, peeled and
roughly chopped

1 litre (34 fl oz/4 cups) chicken stock (see left)

3 tablespoons single (light) cream (35% fat)

1 tablespoon finely snipped fresh chives,
parsley or coriander (cilantro)

> **Baby's serve:** For a young baby, you can thicken this soup with a little rice cereal so that it's easier to spoonfeed. If you don't mind a little mess, you can serve it to your older baby with toast fingers and let her have a try using her own short-handled spoon.
>
> **Toddler's serve:** If your toddler is still mastering the use of her spoon, you can serve this soup in a two-handled mug with some toast fingers.

Melt the butter in a large saucepan over medium heat and cook the onion, garlic and bacon for 3–4 minutes or until the onion is soft. Add the nutmeg and fry gently for 1 minute. Add the pumpkin and stock. Bring to the boil, then reduce the heat and simmer, covered, for about 20 minutes or until the pumpkin is tender.

Using a hand-held blender, purée the soup in the pan. Alternatively, you can purée in several batches in a food processor or blender and then return to the pan.

Stir through the cream and herbs and, if necessary, gently reheat. Serve warm.

* Suitable for freezing

CHICKEN AND SWEETCORN SOUP
SERVES 4

• ı •

You've no doubt enjoyed this satin-textured soup at a Chinese restaurant, but the home-cooked version tastes even better.

1 litre (34 fl oz/4 cups) chicken stock (page 190)

300 g (10½ oz) chicken breast, finely diced

410 g (14 oz) can creamed corn

1 teaspoon soy sauce or tamari

1 tablespoon cornflour (cornstarch)

2 egg whites, lightly whisked

3 spring onions (scallions), thinly sliced

1 teaspoon sesame oil, plus extra, to serve (optional)

small handful of coriander (cilantro) leaves, to serve

> **Baby's serve:** For a young baby, blend the soup to a smooth consistency so that it can be spoon fed. You may need to thicken with a little rice cereal. For an older baby, keep some more texture when blending. If you don't mind the mess, older babies might also like to try their own spoon and some toast fingers.
>
> **Toddler's serve:** A younger toddler may like a two-handled mug and some toast fingers, while an older toddler can probably manage with his own spoon.

Heat the stock in a saucepan and stir in the chicken, corn and soy sauce. Heat gently, stirring.

Meanwhile, mix the cornflour with 2 tablespoons water in a small bowl. When the soup reaches boiling point, add the cornflour mixture, stirring until thickened, about 1 minute.

Stir through the egg white, spring onion and sesame oil. Ladle the soup into serving bowls and sprinkle with coriander leaves. Drizzle your serving with a little extra sesame oil, if you like.

* Suitable for freezing

PEA AND HAM SOUP

SERVES 4–6

This is a dish that our frugal great-grandmothers might have made. It is inexpensive, yet a very comforting and nutritious meal for the whole family. If you have leftovers, you can freeze it for up to a month.

You might also like to stir through a couple of spoonfuls of cream and, for your own serving, some salt and freshly ground black pepper.

500 g (1 lb 2 oz) dried green split peas
1 tablespoon light olive oil
1 onion, diced
3 carrots, peeled and diced
1 garlic clove, diced
2 teaspoons ground turmeric
1 ham hock
2 tablespoons chopped fresh herbs, such as parsley, chives or coriander (cilantro)

Rinse and drain the split peas, then place in a large saucepan with 2 litres (68 fl oz/8 cups) water. Bring to the boil, then reduce the heat and simmer for about 40 minutes or until tender.

Heat the oil in a large saucepan over low–medium heat. Add the onion, carrot and garlic. Cook, stirring, for 6–7 minutes or until the onion is soft but not brown. Stir through the turmeric.

Drain the split peas and add to the onion mixture with the ham hock and 1.5 litres (51 fl oz/6 cups) water. Bring to the boil, then reduce the heat and simmer, covered, for 1 hour.

Transfer the ham hock to a chopping board. Remove the meat, discarding the skin and fat, and cut into small dice. Set aside. Using a hand-held blender, purée the soup to the desired consistency. Add the ham and stir in the chopped herbs. Serve warm.

* Suitable for freezing

Baby's serve: For a young baby, you'll need to blend the ham in with the rest of the soup (or serve the soup without the ham) and then thicken with a little rice cereal to make spoonfeeding easier. Older babies might like to try their own spoon (expect a mess) and some toast fingers.

Toddler's serve: A younger toddler may find it easiest to sip this soup from a two-handled mug and use toast fingers, while an older toddler can probably manage with her own spoon.

MINESTRONE

SERVES 4–6

If your child is not sure about eating a bowl filled with lots of different vegetables, you can blend this soup and serve it with grated cheese on top and toast fingers for dipping.

1 tablespoon olive oil

2 bacon rashers, rind removed and diced

2 garlic cloves, diced

1 onion, diced

1 large carrot, diced

2 celery stalks, diced

2 tablespoons tomato paste

3 tomatoes, diced

1.25 litres (42 fl oz/5 cups) beef, Chicken or Vegetable stock (page 190)

115 g (4 oz/¾ cup) small pasta shells or macaroni

155 g (5 oz/1 cup) fresh or frozen peas

1 zucchini (courgette), diced

150 g (5 oz) green beans, cut into short lengths

400 g (14 oz) can cannellini beans, drained and rinsed

30 g (1 oz/½ cup) chopped parsley

grated parmesan, to serve

Heat the oil in a large saucepan over medium heat and sauté the bacon, garlic, onion, carrot and celery for 4–5 minutes or until the onion is tender. Add the tomato paste and tomatoes and sauté for a further minute. Stir in the stock and 500 ml (17 fl oz/2 cups) water. Bring to the boil, then reduce the heat and simmer, covered, for 40 minutes.

Add the pasta, peas, zucchini, green beans and cannellini beans and simmer, covered, for a further 15 minutes or until the pasta is tender. Scatter over the parsley and parmesan and serve.

* Suitable for freezing

Baby's serve: For a young baby, blend the soup to a smooth consistency so that it's not too lumpy and easier to spoonfeed. For your older baby, keep some lumps when blending or simply give him a bowl with the pasta and vegetables for him to eat as finger food.

Toddler's serve: If your toddler struggles to feed himself soup with a spoon, encourage him to eat the pasta and vegetables with his fingers and use toast fingers for dipping into the broth.

NIÇOISE SALAD

SERVES 4

• I • I • I • I • I • I • I • I • I • I • I • I • I • I • I • I • I • I • I • I • I • I • I • I • I • I •

I love niçoise salad, but my son – like many other young children – is not a fan of boiled potatoes, so I use roasted sweet potato instead.

If your child won't eat green beans, you can substitute them with canned cannellini beans, which many children prefer. Simply rinse and drain the beans before adding to the salad.

1 sweet potato, peeled and diced
3½ tablespoons olive oil
200 g (7 oz) green beans, halved crossways
4 eggs
425 g (15 oz) can tuna, drained
250 g (9 oz) cherry tomatoes, halved
50 g (2 oz/⅓ cup) pitted kalamata olives
3 tablespoons lemon juice

> **Baby's serve:** For a young baby, blend together some of the sweet potato, green beans, tuna, egg and olive oil, adding enough water to achieve a suitable consistency. An older baby can have her own serving for a lovely finger food meal.
>
> **Toddler's serve:** Your toddler should be able to eat this salad with her hands or a spoon or fork.

Preheat the oven to 200°C (400°F). Place the sweet potato in a baking dish and toss through 2 teaspoons of the oil. Roast for about 30 minutes or until tender.

Meanwhile, cook the beans in a saucepan of boiling water until tender, then rinse under cold water, drain and set aside.

Cook the eggs until hard-boiled, about 6 minutes. Rinse under cold water, peel and cut into quarters.

Combine the roasted sweet potato and beans in a large bowl with the tuna, tomatoes, olives, lemon juice and remaining oil. Toss until combined. Divide among serving plates and top with the egg quarters.

> If there are ingredients in this salad that you know your child won't eat, give them to her anyway. The best way to overcome picky eating is to keep offering a variety of ingredients and not make a big deal of your child's rejection. Don't stress if she won't touch them. Just seeing different ingredients and having them on her plate – as well as watching you eat them – are important steps in overcoming fussiness. So even if they're not eaten, they will have served an important purpose. One day she may just surprise you and start munching on that green bean she usually can't stand!

SNEAKY MACARONI CHEESE

SERVES 4

Sneaking vegetables into children's meals actually goes against my core philosophy of cooking for children. I passionately believe children need to regularly see and taste vegetables in their whole form in order to form a liking for them. However, I recognise that sometimes hidden vegetables are a useful tool for improving the diet of a fussy toddler.

This macaroni cheese is seriously good and I would very happily eat it myself any night of the week. Keeping some frozen puréed vegetables on hand will mean you can whip it up in no time at all. If you don't have one of the purées in this recipe handy, just substitute with another vegetable purée.

> **Baby's serve:** For a young baby, blend the macaroni cheese to a smooth consistency, adding a little extra milk or water if needed. For an older baby, you may need to cut up the pasta a little, or he may eat it as finger food.
>
> **Toddler's serve:** Simply serve as is.

300 g (10½ oz/2 cups) macaroni

30 g (1 oz) butter

2 tablespoons plain (all-purpose) flour

500 ml (17 fl oz/2 cups) milk

100 g (3½ oz) ham, diced, optional

125 ml (4 fl oz/½ cup) cauliflower purée (page 84)

125 ml (4 fl oz/½ cup) pumpkin purée (page 84)

125 ml (4 fl oz/½ cup) spinach purée (page 84)

90 g (3 oz/¾ cup) grated gruyère or cheddar cheese

50 g (2 oz/½ cup) grated parmesan, plus extra, to serve

Cook the macaroni according to the instructions on the packet. Drain and set aside.

Melt the butter in a saucepan over low heat. Stir in the flour and cook for 1 minute. Gradually add the milk, stirring over low–medium heat until the sauce thickens.

Gently stir in the ham, purées, cheeses and macaroni and cook for 1 minute. Serve warm, sprinkled with parmesan.

* Suitable for freezing

> When serving 'hidden vegetables', you can also include a visible vegetable – perhaps a side of carrots, or you could stir through some frozen peas – so your child is reminded that vegetables are always part of dinnertime.

PUMPKIN AND PEA RISOTTO

SERVES 4

• •

The secret to a good risotto is using a flavoursome, homemade stock. Risotto is a great family meal because you can serve it for dinner with a big green salad, and then roll any cold leftovers into balls for your baby or toddler to have as finger food the next day.

You might also like to stir through some chopped pine nuts or baby spinach, or even a little mascarpone or cream if that will make the dish more enticing to your child.

400 g (14 oz) diced pumpkin

2 tablespoons olive oil

750 ml (25 fl oz/3 cups) vegetable or chicken stock (page 190)

20 g (¾ oz) butter

4–6 spring onions (scallions) or 1 small onion, thinly sliced

330 g (12 oz/1½ cups) arborio rice

1 garlic clove, crushed

80 g (3 oz/½ cup) frozen peas

juice of 1 lemon

35 g (1 oz/⅓ cup) grated parmesan, plus extra, to serve

2 tablespoons finely snipped chives

Preheat the oven to 220°C (430°F). Place the pumpkin in a baking dish, drizzle with the olive oil and roast for about 25 minutes or until tender.

Combine the stock with 375 ml (12½ fl oz/1½ cups) water in a saucepan and bring to the boil. Reduce the heat and simmer, covered. (The stock should be kept simmering the whole time the risotto is cooking).

Melt the butter in a large saucepan over low heat. Add the spring onion and cook, stirring, for about 3 minutes or until soft but not brown. Add the rice and garlic and cook, stirring constantly, for a further minute. Add 250 ml (8½ fl oz/1 cup) of the hot stock and cook, stirring, until the liquid is absorbed.

Continue adding the hot stock, 250 ml (8½ fl oz/1 cup) at a time, stirring continuously. Wait until the stock has been absorbed before adding more (the total cooking time will be about 25 minutes). Continue to stir until the stock is absorbed and the rice is tender. You can add a little more stock or hot water if required.

Stir through the peas and leave for a few minutes to cook through. Add the roast pumpkin, lemon juice, parmesan and chives. Serve sprinkled with extra parmesan.

* Suitable for freezing

Baby's serve: For a young baby, blend the risotto to a smooth consistency, adding a little extra liquid if needed. An older baby should be able to manage as is, although you may need to cut up the pumpkin and peas a little.

Toddler's serve: Simply serve as is.

VEGETABLE PASTA SAUCE

SERVES 6

• | • | • | • | • | • | • | • | • | • | • | • | • | •

This nutritious sauce is so versatile – stir it through hot pasta, mix it with potato mash, use it as a pizza sauce or turn it into homemade baked beans (page 148).

1 tablespoon light olive oil
1 onion, diced
1 garlic clove, halved
1 large carrot, diced
150 g (5 oz/1 cup) diced pumpkin
1 tablespoon tomato paste
1 zucchini (courgette), diced
4–6 button mushrooms, sliced
400 g (14 oz) can no-added-salt chopped
   tomatoes
4 tomatoes, diced
1 teaspoon soft brown sugar (optional)
small handful fresh basil or oregano

Heat the oil in a large saucepan over medium heat. Cook the onion, garlic, carrot and pumpkin, stirring occasionally, for 6–8 minutes or until the onion is soft but not brown. Stir in the tomato paste, then add the zucchini, mushroom, tomatoes and sugar. Simmer, covered, stirring occasionally, for 20 minutes or until the vegetables are tender.

Add the herbs, then purée the sauce using a hand-held blender or food processor. For a thicker sauce, return to the heat and simmer until reduced to your liking.

* Suitable for freezing

SPAGHETTI BOLOGNESE

MAKES ABOUT 7 CUPS

• | • | • | • | • | • | • | • | • | • | • | • | • | •

If your child is not a great vegetable eater, this bolognese provides an easy way of including a few more in her diet. I like to keep some in the freezer so it's ready and waiting on those nights when I need a quick, easy meal.

2 teaspoons olive oil
500 g (1 lb 2 oz) minced (ground) beef
1 quantity vegetable pasta sauce (see left)
500 g (1 lb 2 oz) spaghetti or pasta shapes
parmesan shavings, to serve

Heat the oil in a large frying pan and brown the beef, stirring to break up the lumps. Set aside.

Prepare the pasta sauce as directed, adding the browned beef with the tomatoes. Continue as directed, simmering the sauce for an additional 5–10 minutes.

Cook the pasta according to the instructions on the packet. Drain and toss through the bolognese sauce. Sprinkle with parmesan to serve.

* Suitable for freezing

Baby's serve: For a young baby, blend the spaghetti bolognese to a smooth consistency. For an older baby, cut up the spaghetti so that it can be easily eaten with a spoon.

Toddler's serve: Serve as is or cut up the spaghetti so that she can self-feed with a spoon.

'With its gentle taste, most babies and toddlers will accept cauliflower in one form or another. Mashed or puréed, it can be added to soups, meatballs and pasta dishes for a wonderful nutritional boost.'

FARFALLE WITH CAULIFLOWER AND BREADCRUMBS

SERVES 4

We all have those moments when the fridge is bare, except for perhaps a cauliflower in the crisper. Don't call your local Italian. This dish is a million times better than any takeaway, plus it will make you feel oh-so-resourceful.

125 ml (4 fl oz/½ cup) extra-virgin olive oil
40 g (1½ oz/½ cup) fresh breadcrumbs
½ cauliflower, cut into small florets
2 garlic cloves, thinly sliced
375 g (13 oz) farfalle pasta
155 g (5 oz/1 cup) fresh or frozen peas
75 g (2½ oz) butter
75 g (2½ oz/¾ cup) grated parmesan,
    plus extra, to serve
2 tablespoons chopped fresh basil or mint

Heat half the olive oil in a large frying pan over medium heat and cook the breadcrumbs for about 5 minutes or until golden (take care not to burn them). Remove and set aside.

Wipe out the pan, heat the remaining oil and cook the cauliflower, turning regularly, for 7–8 minutes or until golden and almost cooked through. Add the garlic and cook for a further 1–2 minutes or until soft.

Meanwhile, cook the pasta according to the instructions on the packet, adding the peas for the final 1–2 minutes of cooking (fresh peas will take a little longer). Drain, leaving the pasta quite wet so that it adds moisture to the dish, and return to the saucepan.

Add the cauliflower with the butter and parmesan and toss until the butter has melted. Stir through the herbs and breadcrumbs. Serve topped with extra parmesan.

Baby's serve: Set aside a serving for baby, being particularly generous with the cauliflower and peas, and blend with a little water to an appropriate consistency (you can freeze any leftover baby portions if you like). An older baby can eat this dish simply as is with his hands.

Toddler's serve: This is perfect toddler finger food and doesn't need any variation. Make sure your toddler gets plenty of the vegetables.

Making breadcrumbs: Just take your leftover stale bread, cut off the crusts, chop it up into rough chunks and blend in the food processor or blender until you have breadcrumbs. You can freeze any extra to use later.

If you're using fresh bread (which will be too moist to blend), cut it into slices, remove the crusts, and bake in a 150°C (300°F) oven for 15 minutes to dry it out. You can then chop it up and pop in the food processor.

RATATOUILLE

SERVES 6

• •

This is a dish our family never tires of. It's delicious with a piece of grilled fish, lamb or steak, and also makes a beautiful omelette filling. My local Italian grocer makes it with potato, which is definitely not traditional, but I love it. I've borrowed his idea for this recipe.

80 ml (3 fl oz/⅓ cup) olive oil
2 onions, finely diced
1 large potato (desiree or similar variety), peeled and diced
1 eggplant (aubergine), diced
2 red capsicums (peppers), cut into squares
3 zucchini (courgettes), thickly sliced
2 garlic cloves, sliced
4 ripe tomatoes, cut into eighths
3 tablespoons pitted black olives
2 tablespoons chopped fresh basil or parsley
extra-virgin olive oil and grated parmesan, to serve

Heat the oil in a saucepan over medium heat and cook the onion and potato for 5 minutes or until the onion is soft and light golden. Add the eggplant, capsicum, zucchini and garlic and cook for 5 minutes. Add the tomato, cover and gently simmer for 20 minutes or until the vegetables are tender. If you would like the sauce to reduce and thicken a little, simmer it, uncovered, for a further 10 minutes.

Stir through the olives, scatter over the basil and serve with a drizzle of olive oil and some grated parmesan.

Baby's serve: For a younger baby, remove the olives (which are a bit salty for a young baby's kidneys to cope with) and blend to an appropriate consistency. You can freeze any leftover baby portions. For an older baby, cut up to a consistency that can be easily eaten with a spoon. You might like to stir through some mashed potato, rice or pasta and top with grated cheese.

Toddler's serve: Serve as for an older baby, above, or simply as is.

'Canned legumes are an absolute saviour for time-poor parents – simply rinse and drain for a fantastic finger-food snack.'

CHILLI CON CARNE

SERVES 4–6

There's not much you can't do with chilli con carne. Make it a filling for tacos, tortillas or puff pastry, or a topping for nachos or jacket potatoes, or even just serve it warm on wholegrain toast with salad for a simple lunch or dinner.

Depending on how many people there are in your family, you might like to freeze half the chilli con carne for another meal.

1 tablespoon light olive oil

1 onion, finely diced

1 carrot, finely diced

1 red capsicum (pepper), finely diced

2 garlic cloves, crushed

500 g (1 lb 2 oz) minced (ground) beef

1 teaspoon sweet paprika

1 teaspoon ground cumin

½ teaspoon dried oregano

3 tablespoons tomato paste

400 g (14 oz) can no-added-salt chopped tomatoes

400 g (14 oz) can red kidney beans

2 tablespoons finely chopped fresh coriander (cilantro) (optional)

Heat the oil in a large saucepan over medium heat. Cook the onion, carrot, capsicum and garlic, stirring, for about 5 minutes or until the onion is soft but not brown.

Add the beef and cook, stirring, for about 5 minutes or until browned. Stir through the spices and oregano and cook for a further minute. Add the tomato paste, canned tomatoes and 250 ml (8½ fl oz/1 cup) water. Reduce the heat and simmer, covered, for about 15 minutes.

Remove the lid and simmer for a further 5 minutes, adding the kidney beans and coriander 1 minute before the end of the cooking time.

* Suitable for freezing

> **Baby's serve:** For a younger baby, blend to an appropriate consistency. For an older baby, cut up to a consistency that can be easily eaten with a spoon. You might like to stir through mashed potato, rice or pasta.
>
> **Toddler's serve:** Serve as for an older baby, above, or simply as is.

RED LENTIL, PUMPKIN AND COCONUT DAL

SERVES 4

· | · | · | · | · | · | · | · | · | · | · | · | · | · | · | · | · | · | · | · | · | · | · | · | · | · | · | · | · | ·

This lovely dal is very mild, so don't worry if your child isn't accustomed to spices. The coconut milk gives it a delicious creaminess.

2 teaspoons light olive oil

1 onion, finely diced

1 teaspoon finely grated fresh ginger

80 g (3 oz/½ cup) finely diced carrot

¼ teaspoon ground cumin

¼ teaspoon ground coriander

¼ teaspoon ground turmeric

250 g (9 oz/1 cup) split red lentils, rinsed and drained

270 ml (9 fl oz) can coconut milk

310 g (11 oz/2 cups) diced pumpkin

125 g (4 oz/1 cup) diced cauliflower

155 g (5 oz/1 cup) fresh or frozen peas

2 tablespoons lemon juice

1 tablespoon finely chopped fresh coriander (cilantro)

cooked basmati rice, to serve

Heat the oil in a large saucepan over low heat. Add the onion, ginger and carrot and cook for about 5 minutes or until the onion is soft but not brown. Stir in the spices and lentils and cook for a further 2 minutes.

Add the coconut milk and 435 ml (15 fl oz/1¾ cups) water. Cover and simmer for 5 minutes. Stir through the pumpkin, cauliflower and peas and simmer, covered, for another 20 minutes or until the vegetables are tender.

Remove from the heat and stir through the lemon juice and coriander. Serve with basmati rice.

* Suitable for freezing

> Baby's serve: Blend together some dal and rice until smooth. For an older baby, cut up the dal to a consistency that can be easily eaten with a spoon and stir through some of the rice.
>
> Toddler's serve: Serve as for an older baby, above.

> Lentils are a good source of protein and also count towards one of your child's (and your) daily servings of vegetables.
>
> Many adults falsely believe that if we don't eat meat every day, we're not getting enough protein. However, plant sources such as legumes, nuts and seeds also provide protein, as well as plenty of fibre and other important nutrients. If your child eats eggs and dairy products, these are another protein source. So don't feel you need to give your child meat every day. Nutrient-dense vegetarian meals like this will do her the world of good.

FISH AND RISONI STEW

SERVES 4

It is so important to include fish in your child's diet. It's low in saturated fat and packed with healthy nutrients, including the all-important omega-3s. Also, there is some evidence that children who eat plenty of fish are less likely to develop asthma.

This is one of my grandma's recipes that my son loves. It's a fabulous, quick meal for a busy weeknight.

1 tablespoon light olive oil

1 small leek, thinly sliced

2 carrots, peeled and diced

2 garlic cloves, crushed

400 g (14 oz) can no-added-salt cherry or chopped tomatoes

2 tablespoons lemon juice

165 g (6 oz/¾ cup) risoni

pinch of saffron threads, optional

600 g (1 lb 5 oz) firm white fish fillets, bones removed and cut into chunks

15 g (½ oz/½ cup) finely chopped flat-leaf parsley

crusty bread and salad, to serve

> **Baby's serve:** Blend together your younger baby's serving until smooth (you can freeze any leftover baby portions if you like). For an older baby, cut up to a consistency that can be easily eaten with a spoon.
>
> **Toddler's serve:** Serve as for an older baby, above, or simply as is.

Heat the oil in a heavy-based saucepan over medium heat. Cook the leek, carrot and garlic for 5 minutes or until the leek is soft but not brown. Add the tomato, lemon juice and 500 ml (17 fl oz/2 cups) water and bring to the boil.

Add the risoni and saffron, reduce the heat and simmer, stirring occasionally, for 10–12 minutes or until the risoni is just cooked.

Add the fish, cover and simmer gently for 5–6 minutes or until the fish is cooked through. Stir through the parsley.

Serve warm, with bread and salad on the side.

> When selecting fish, remember that some species are more sustainable than others. It's worth contacting your national marine conservation society (for example, see www.sustainableseafood.org.au in Australia) to find out the sustainable species in your country. Following their advice helps ensure that your children's children will also be able to enjoy fish for dinner.

MEDITERRANEAN BAKED FISH

SERVES 4

• •

This dish is impressive enough for a dinner party, but also simple enough for an easy weeknight meal.

6 potatoes (desiree or similar variety), peeled
4 zucchini (courgettes)
2 onions
3 tablespoons olive oil
4 white fish fillets (about 800 g/1 lb 12 oz), bones removed
12–18 cherry tomatoes
3 tablespoons pitted black olives
½ bunch flat-leaf parsley or chives, finely chopped (optional)
lemon wedges, to serve

Preheat the oven to 180°C (350°F). Using a mandolin, slice the potatoes, zucchini and onions very finely (you can do this by hand if you don't have a mandolin).

Spread the potato and onion evenly in a large baking dish. Drizzle half the olive oil evenly over the vegetables and bake for 15 minutes. Toss through the zucchini and bake for 15 minutes or until the potato is turning golden and almost cooked.

Place the fish fillets on top of the vegetables. Scatter the tomatoes and olives around the fish. Drizzle the remaining olive oil evenly over the top. Return to the oven and bake for 15 minutes or until the fish is cooked through and the vegetables are tender. Scatter the herbs on top and serve with wedges of lemon.

> **Baby's serve:** Set aside some of the vegetables and fish (without olives, which are too salty for a young baby), and blend with a little water to an appropriate consistency. If you wish, you can freeze any leftover baby portions. An older baby can eat this dish simply as is with her hands.
>
> **Toddler's serve:** This is great toddler finger food and doesn't need any variation. Don't assume your toddler won't want a squeeze of lemon on hers. Offer it to her and let her decide. Children typically have a stronger preference for sour tastes than adults – she might love it given the chance.

CHICKEN SCHNITZEL WITH FIVE-BEAN SALAD

SERVES 4

The addition of parmesan, lemon and herbs to the breadcrumbs makes this schnitzel absolutely delicious. It will expose your child to a more complex set of flavours than a traditional schnitzel – great for developing his little palate. If you have a fussy eater, you can leave these extras out.

The honey dressing is really tasty, but because of the risk of botulism from the honey, it's not suitable for a baby under 12 months.

4 chicken breast fillets (about 700 g/1 lb 7 oz)
50 g (2 oz/⅓ cup) plain (all-purpose) flour
160 g (6 oz/2 cups) fresh breadcrumbs
20 g (¾ oz/⅓ cup) finely chopped fresh herbs, such as parsley, basil and thyme or oregano
35 g (1 oz/⅓ cup) finely grated parmesan
1 teaspoon finely grated lemon rind
2 eggs
1 tablespoon milk
light olive oil, for shallow-frying

Five-bean salad
310 g (11 oz/2 cups) frozen broad (fava) beans
400 g (14 oz) can no-added-salt four-bean mix, rinsed and drained
creamy honey dressing (page 226)

Cut each chicken breast in half by placing your palm on top and carefully running the knife through the centre of the fillet. Place each chicken piece between two sheets of plastic wrap (cling film) and gently pound with a meat mallet until about 5 mm (¼ in) thick.

Place the flour on a plate. Combine the breadcrumbs, herbs, parmesan and lemon rind in a shallow bowl. In another shallow bowl, lightly beat together the eggs and milk. Coat the chicken pieces in the flour, then in the egg mixture, then the breadcrumb mixture. Refrigerate until required.

To make the salad, cook the broad beans in a saucepan of boiling water for 4 minutes or until tender. Refresh under cold running water, then drain, peel and discard the skins. Combine the broad beans, mixed beans and dressing.

Heat the oil in a large frying pan over medium–high heat. Cook the chicken until golden brown on both sides and cooked through. Drain on paper towels. Serve with the bean salad.

> **Baby's serve:** Remember that babies can't have honey (see page 42), so don't give any of the dressing to your baby. For a younger baby, blend some of the schnitzel and beans with a little water.
>
> For an older baby, cut the schnitzel into strips for finger food. He may be able to pick up the beans or you may need to chop them up for spoonfeeding. If you're concerned about the beans being a choking hazard for your child, mash them with a fork.
>
> **Toddler's serve:** With the schnitzel cut into strips, this is great finger food and doesn't need any variation.

ONE-POT CHICKEN

SERVES 4

• •

This dish is one of our family staples. The lemon gives it a lovely lift and there's plenty of sauce, so you might like to serve it with some crusty bread to mop up the delicious juices.

Your butcher can cut the chicken into pieces for you. If you prefer, you can use four chicken legs and four chicken thighs on the bone. You can also vary the vegetables – brussels sprouts and green beans also work well. Just add them to the pot according to the cooking time they require.

1 chicken, cut into eight pieces

3 tablespoons plain (all-purpose) flour

2 tablespoons olive oil

2 large carrots, thickly sliced

1 onion, diced

1 garlic clove, diced

4 potatoes, peeled and quartered

1 red capsicum (pepper), cut into thick strips

1 lemon, cut in half

2 zucchini (courgettes), sliced

½ bunch parsley, finely chopped

Dust the chicken pieces in the flour. Heat the oil in a large flameproof casserole dish over medium–high heat. Cook the chicken pieces, turning, for about 5 minutes or until browned but not cooked through. You may need to do this in batches. Remove the chicken from the dish and set aside.

Reduce the heat, add the carrot, onion and garlic and cook for 5 minutes or until the onion is soft. Add the leg and thigh pieces, potato, capsicum, lemon (giving a good squeeze as you do) and 185 ml (6 fl oz/¾ cup) water. Cover and cook for 20 minutes.

Add the wing and breast pieces and zucchini. Cook, covered, for a further 15 minutes or until the chicken is cooked through and the vegetables are tender. Remove the lemon halves and scatter the parsley on top.

Baby's serve: Take some chicken off the bone and blend with vegetables and some of the sauce to an appropriate consistency (you can freeze any leftover blended portions). For an older baby, cut into smaller pieces that can be easily eaten with a spoon. Your older baby might like to eat the chicken straight off one of the leg bones (watch out for any sharp splinters).

Toddler's serve: Serve as you would for an older baby or simply as is. You may need to peel the skin off the capsicum strips.

BEEF AND SWEET POTATO COTTAGE PIE

SERVES 4–6

● ı ●

This is the kind of favourite meal that has a grown son reminiscing about his mum's cooking. Someday it might just tempt your baby back home for the occasional family meal when he's all grown up.

The sweet potato topping provides a more nutritious and lower-gi meal than the traditional potato topping. You can serve it in a large dish or in individual ramekins. Since there are three of us in our family, I divide the mixture between two ovenproof dishes so we have one for dinner and one to freeze for another occasion.

1 tablespoon light olive oil, plus extra, for drizzling

1 onion, finely diced

1 carrot, peeled and finely diced

2 celery stalks, finely diced

500 g (1 lb 2 oz) minced (ground) beef

2 tablespoons tomato paste

400 g (14 oz) can no-added-salt chopped tomatoes

235 g (8 oz/1½ cups) frozen peas

2 tablespoons chopped parsley

700 g (1 lb 7 oz) sweet potato, peeled and diced

20 g (¾ oz) butter

60 g (2 oz/½ cup) grated cheddar cheese

Preheat the oven to 180°C (350°F). Heat the oil in a large saucepan over medium heat. Add the onion, carrot and celery and cook, stirring, for 5 minutes or until the onion has softened. Add the beef. Cook, stirring with a wooden spoon to break up any lumps, for 5 minutes or until the beef has browned.

Stir in the tomato paste, chopped tomato and 185 ml (6 fl oz/¾ cup) water. Simmer for 10 minutes or until the sauce has thickened. Stir in the peas and parsley.

Meanwhile, cook the sweet potato in a saucepan of boiling water for 10–15 minutes or until tender. Drain and return to the pan. Mash until smooth, then stir through the butter.

Spoon the beef mixture into a 2 litre (68 fl oz/8 cup) ovenproof dish (or two or more smaller dishes). Top with the sweet potato mixture. Sprinkle with the cheese and a very light drizzle of oil. Bake for 25 minutes or until the top is lightly browned.

* Suitable for freezing

> **Baby's serve:** For a younger baby, blend together the cottage pie filling and topping (you may need to add a little water) to an appropriate consistency. For an older baby, chop up to a consistency that can be easily eaten with a spoon.
>
> **Toddler's serve:** Chop up a little as you would for an older baby or simply serve as is.

MELT-IN-THE-MOUTH BEEF CASSEROLE

SERVES 4–6

· ·

This is adapted from an old recipe of my mum's that our family has been making for many years. It's a great one to prepare while your child is having a daytime sleep – you can just let it sit and bubble away on the stove, getting richer and more melt-in-the-mouth as time passes.

1 kg (2 lb 3 oz) stewing beef, such as cheek, chuck, gravy or blade steak

2 tablespoons olive oil

8 baby onions, peeled and halved

2 tablespoons plain (all-purpose) flour

2 garlic cloves, diced

few sprigs thyme

1 bay leaf

3 carrots, quartered

250 g (9 oz) cherry tomatoes

310 g (11 oz/2 cups) frozen peas

3 tablespoons chopped parsley

potato or Three-vegetable mash (page 220), to serve

Cut the beef into 4 cm (1½ in) cubes. Heat the oil in a large flameproof casserole dish over medium heat and cook the onions for a few minutes, until golden brown but not cooked through. Remove and set aside.

Increase the heat and brown the beef in batches, turning frequently. Return all the beef to the pan and sprinkle with the flour. Cook, stirring, for a few minutes until the flour has browned. Stir in the garlic, herbs and 500 ml (17 fl oz/2 cups) water. Bring to the boil, then reduce the heat to low, cover and simmer for 1½ hours.

Add the carrot, tomatoes and browned onions, cover and cook for 20 minutes. Add the peas and cook for a further 3 minutes or until the beef and vegetables are tender. Remove the bay leaf and scatter the parsley on top. Serve with potato or three-vegetable mash.

Baby's serve: For a younger baby, blend together some of the beef, vegetables and sauce to an appropriate consistency (you can freeze any leftover blended portions). For an older baby, mash or chop up a little so that it can be easily eaten with a spoon.

Toddler's serve: Chop up a little as you would for an older baby or simply serve as is and allow your toddler to eat with her hands and her own spoon or fork.

You may be tempted to make this beef casserole with red wine. However, cooking does not remove all of the alcohol from wine or spirits. The amount of alcohol remaining depends on the cooking method and time. An alcoholic drink stirred through a liquid dish (like a casserole) and simmered for 15 minutes retains about 40 per cent alcohol. Cooking that dish for two hours will leave 10 per cent of the alcohol. For more information, see the USDA Table of Nutrient Retention Factors at www.ars.usda.gov/nutrientdata.

SLOW-COOKED LAMB SHANKS

SERVES 4

• ı • ı

Make this superb dish once and I've no doubt it will become one that you treasure forever, with its succulent, falling-off-the-bone meat. It's another good one to make earlier in the day, during one of those precious baby nap times. Simply reheat it on the stovetop and stir through the cannellini beans before serving.

4 french-trimmed lamb shanks
3 tablespoons plain (all-purpose) flour
2 tablespoons light olive oil
1 onion, finely diced
1 celery stalk, sliced
2 garlic cloves, crushed
1 tablespoon balsamic vinegar
400 g (14 oz) can no-added-salt chopped tomatoes
2 anchovy fillets, finely chopped
3 carrots, halved lengthways and cut into thirds
4 sprigs thyme
400 g (14 oz) can cannellini beans, drained and rinsed
1 tablespoon finely chopped parsley
mashed potato and steamed green vegetables, to serve

Preheat the oven to 180°C (350°F). Lightly dust the lamb shanks with the flour.

Heat half of the oil in a large flameproof casserole dish over medium–high heat. Add the lamb shanks and cook, turning, for a few minutes until golden brown. Set aside.

Reduce the heat and add the remaining oil to the pan. Add the onion and cook over low heat for 5 minutes or until the onion has softened. Add the celery and garlic and cook for 1 minute.

Increase the heat, add the balsamic vinegar and boil briskly for a few seconds. Add the tomato and 250 ml (8½ fl oz/1 cup) water and return to the boil. Add the anchovies and carrot, then return the lamb shanks to the pan and scatter over the thyme. Cover with a lid (or tightly with foil) and cook in the oven for 1½–2 hours or until the meat is very tender.

Remove the lid and return to the oven, uncovered, for a further 15 minutes. Stir through the cannellini beans and leave for 1 minute to warm through. Sprinkle with parsley and serve with mashed potato and green vegetables.

Baby's serve: For a younger baby, cut some lamb off the shank and blend with some carrot and sauce until smooth (if you like, you can freeze any leftover blended portions). For an older baby, mash or cut up into smaller pieces that can be eaten with a spoon.

Toddler's serve: Cut the lamb into strips for finger food or for your toddler to eat with a fork, and serve with the carrot, beans and steamed green vegetables.

LAMB CUTLETS WITH THREE-VEGETABLE MASH

SERVES 4

• •

Cutlets are a great baby and toddler food as they have their own handle – perfect for little hands. Chewing on the bone is also good for your child's developing teeth and gums.

If your child is not usually a zucchini (courgette) fan, this delicious mash may convert him. The zucchini is grated and stirred through right at the end, so it's not overcooked and soggy, like zucchini so often is.

400 g (14 oz) sweet potato, peeled and
   cut into large chunks

1 garlic clove

500 g (1 lb 2 oz) cauliflower, cut into
   large chunks

40 g (1½ oz/⅓ cup) grated cheddar cheese
   or a mixture of cheddar and parmesan

1 zucchini (courgette), grated

2 teaspoons light olive oil

8–12 lamb cutlets

Lemon parsley sauce

2 tablespoons finely chopped parsley

2 tablespoons extra-virgin olive oil

2 teaspoons lemon juice

Boil or steam the sweet potato and garlic for 4 minutes. Add the cauliflower and cook for a further 7–8 minutes or until the vegetables are tender. Drain and return to the saucepan. Stir through the cheese and purée with a hand-held blender until smooth (alternatively you can use a food processor). Stir through the grated zucchini, return to a gentle heat and cook for a minute until the zucchini is just cooked. Set aside, covered, to keep warm.

To make the lemon parsley sauce, whisk together the parsley, olive oil and lemon juice.

Heat the oil in a frying pan and cook the cutlets over medium heat on both sides until golden brown and cooked to your liking.

Drizzle the sauce over the cutlets and mash to serve.

> **Baby's serve:** For a younger baby, chop up some of the lamb and blend with the mash and parsley sauce until smooth, adding a little water if needed to get the right consistency (leftover blended portions can be frozen for later use). For an older baby, cut up some of the lamb and stir through the mash, giving her the bone with a little meat left on for chewing.
>
> **Toddler's serve:** Cut the lamb into strips for finger food or for your toddler to eat with a fork, and serve with the mash and sauce on the side.

EASY FRIED RICE WITH CHICKEN

SERVES 4

This dish is popular with families the world over, and for good reason: it's easy, nutritious and totally delicious.

I like my fried rice with a very light drizzle of sesame oil over the top, but the flavour may be too strong for your little person. You could give it a go and see what he thinks.

Basmati rice is a good choice because it's one of the lowest-GI rices available, but you can also use regular white rice if that's what is in your pantry.

200 g (7 oz/1 cup) basmati rice
1 tablespoon light olive oil
400 g (14 oz) chicken breast fillet, cut into strips
1 bacon rasher, diced (optional)
150 g (5 oz/1 cup) grated carrot
150 g (5 oz/1 cup) fresh or frozen peas
150 g (5 oz/1 cup) fresh or frozen corn kernels
2 garlic cloves, crushed
2 spring onions (scallions), thinly sliced
2 tablespoons sesame seeds
2 eggs, lightly beaten
2½ tablespoons salt-reduced soy sauce or tamari
3 tablespoons coriander (cilantro) leaves, chopped (optional)

Cook the rice according to the instructions on the packet. Fluff with a fork and set aside to cool.

Heat the oil in a frying pan or wok over high heat and cook the chicken and bacon, stirring, for 4 minutes or until light golden. Add the carrot, peas, corn, garlic, spring onion and sesame seeds and cook for a further 4 minutes. Add the eggs and cook for a further minute or until set.

Stir in the rice and cook, stirring, for 3–4 minutes. Stir through the soy sauce and coriander. Serve immediately.

Baby's serve: Younger babies will need their serve blended, with a little water, to a suitable consistency. For an older baby, cut up to a consistency that can be easily eaten with a spoon or let him have a go at self-feeding with his hands.

Toddler's serve: Your toddler will probably want to eat this by himself with his hands or a spoon.

LEBANESE GREEN BEANS

SERVES 4–6

● | ● | ● | ● | ● | ● | ● | ● | ● | ● | ● | ●

I adore these slow-cooked Lebanese beans. They work really well in a pressure cooker. Try them with some hummus (page 153) on the side.

It's best to use really ripe – even overripe – tomatoes because they'll lend a lovely sweetness to this dish. If your tomatoes aren't as ripe as they could be, add a pinch of sugar instead.

2 tablespoons light olive oil
1 onion, finely diced
500 g (1 lb 2 oz) green beans, halved crossways
1 garlic clove, diced
3 large tomatoes, diced
¼ teaspoon ground allspice

Heat the oil in a saucepan over medium heat and sauté the onion for 5 minutes or until soft but not brown. Stir in the beans and garlic, cover and cook for 5 minutes. Stir through the tomato and allspice and cook, covered, for 30 minutes over low heat. Serve warm or cold.

> **Baby's serve:** For a younger baby, blend some beans and sauce to an appropriate consistency for spoonfeeding, adding a little grated cheddar if you like (leftover portions can be frozen for later use). For an older baby, leave as is for her to eat with her hands, or chop up and top with some grated cheese.
> **Toddler's serve:** Serve as for an older baby, above.

CREAMY POLENTA

SERVES 4

● | ● | ● | ● | ● | ● | ● | ● | ● | ● | ● | ●

Made from cornmeal, polenta makes a perfect baby food and a delicious change from vegetable mash for the rest of the family.

750 ml (25 fl oz/3 cups) milk
100 g (3½ oz/⅔ cup) polenta
60 g (2 oz/½ cup) grated cheddar cheese

Bring the milk and 500 ml (17 fl oz/2 cups) water to the boil in a large saucepan. Gradually add the polenta to the liquid, stirring continuously.

Reduce the heat to very low and simmer, stirring regularly, for about 10 minutes or until the polenta thickens. Stir in the cheese until melted and combined.

* Suitable for freezing

> **Baby's serve:** Serve to baby as is or combined with a vegetable or meat purée.
> **Toddler's serve:** Serve as a side to whichever main dish you've made.

'Corn on the cob makes a wonderful finger food for an older baby and toddler. It's easy for your baby to hold and encourages good chewing development.'

CORN ON THE COB

SERVES 4

• । • । • । • । • । • । • । • । • । • ।

Babies and toddlers can sometimes be very particular about exactly how a food is served. Get it right and they'll devour it. Get it ever-so-slightly wrong and it will be emphatically thrown on the floor. Corn is the perfect example. My son absolutely will not eat it in separate kernels, but hand him the cob and he's as happy as a clam.

3–4 corn cobs
40 g (1½ oz) butter

Steam, boil or microwave the corn until tender. Spread with the butter and allow to cool enough for your child to hold it. Serve cut into three to four pieces for little hands to manage.

> **Baby's serve:** Depending on your baby's age, she may like to have a go with the whole piece of corn or eat the separate kernels with her fingers, which you can cut from the cob. Babies new to solids will probably cope best with the creamy corn and leek purée instead (see right).
>
> **Toddler's serve:** Toddlers typically love having a munch on a cob of corn, so don't feel you need to cut the kernels off. Let your toddler's budding teeth do the work instead.

CREAMY CORN AND LEEK PURÉE

SERVES 4

• । • । • । • । • । • । • । • । • । • ।

For a baby who's too young to munch on a corn cob, this corn purée is just the thing. It's so delicious, you can serve it as a side dish for the whole family. My mum thinks it's the yummiest vegetable dish ever.

3–4 corn cobs
1 tablespoon olive oil
1 small leek, thinly sliced
80 ml (3 fl oz/⅓ cup) water or
  chicken stock (page 190)
80 g (3 oz/⅓ cup) sour cream

Slice the kernels off the corn cobs. Heat the oil in a saucepan over low–medium heat and cook the leek for about 5 minutes or until soft but not brown. Add the corn and water or stock. Cover and simmer, stirring occasionally, for 10 minutes or until the corn is tender. Stir through the sour cream, then transfer to a food processor and blend until smooth.

* Suitable for freezing

> **Baby's serve:** The corn husks in this purée can be a little fibrous for a younger baby. If your baby is under nine months, it's a good idea to pass the purée through a mouli or coarse sieve before serving it as is or combined with a vegetable or meat purée.
>
> **Toddler's serve:** Serve as a side to whichever main dish you've made.

CREAMY HONEY DRESSING

MAKES ABOUT ⅓ CUP

• ı • ı • ı • ı • ı • ı • ı • ı • ı • ı • ı • ı • ı

This dressing is delicious drizzled over avocado, or served as a dipping sauce when you're trying to tempt a toddler to eat his vegetables. However, because of the risk of botulism from the honey, the dressing is not suitable for a baby under 12 months.

2 tablespoons ricotta or spreadable cream
   cheese, softened
1 tablespoon olive oil
2 teaspoons lemon juice
1 tablespoon honey

Whisk together all the ingredients until well combined and smooth.

> **Baby's serve:** This recipe is not suitable for babies under 12 months.
>
> **Toddler's serve:** Serve as is drizzled over salad, legumes, avocado or as a dipping sauce for vegetable sticks.

RAINBOW CHIPS

SERVES 4–6

• ı • ı • ı • ı • ı • ı • ı • ı • ı • ı • ı • ı • ı

If your child likes potato chips, try adding these other vegetables to her chip repertoire.

I confess my son is not a fan of zucchini (courgette) unless it's grated and hidden, but I know plenty of children who will eat it when cooked this way. Thankfully, he adores all the other vegetables in this dish and it's great to know he's getting such good variety.

2 potatoes (desiree or similar variety), peeled
1 sweet potato, peeled
2 parsnips, peeled
2 carrots, peeled
2 zucchini (courgettes)
2 tablespoons olive oil

Preheat the oven to 180°C (350°F). Cut all the vegetables into similar-sized strips and place in a large baking dish. Drizzle with the oil and roast for about 35–40 minutes or until golden.

> **Baby's serve:** For a younger baby, blend with a little water to an appropriate consistency (leftover blended portions can be frozen). For an older baby, this dish is perfect finger food. Alternatively, you can chop it up, top it with a little grated cheese and serve with a spoon.
>
> **Toddler's serve:** Serve as is.

APPLE AND BERRY CRUMBLE

SERVES 4

· ı ·

You can tailor this crumble so it's just the way you like it. If you prefer the fruit soft and mushy, cook it for a little longer on the stovetop, giving it a good stir. If you like to be able to see all the fruity pieces, take it off the heat a bit sooner.

Whenever I make this dish, I try to keep some leftovers so I can warm it up for a sneaky breakfast the next day.

4 apples, peeled and diced
¼ teaspoon ground cinnamon
3 tablespoons soft brown sugar
150 g (5 oz/1 cup) fresh or frozen
   mixed berries
75 g (2½ oz/¾ cup) rolled oats
3 tablespoons plain (all-purpose) flour
60 g (2 oz) butter
Whole-egg custard (page 231),
   to serve (optional)

Preheat the oven to 180°C (350°F). Combine the apple, cinnamon, 2 tablespoons of the sugar and 2 tablespoons of water in a saucepan over low heat. Cover and cook for 10–15 minutes or until the apple is just tender. Remove from the heat and fold through the berries.

Combine the rolled oats, flour and remaining brown sugar in a bowl. Using your fingertips, rub in the butter until well combined.

Transfer the fruit mixture to a 1.5 litre (51 fl oz/6 cup) ovenproof dish. Sprinkle over the oat mixture. Bake for about 20–25 minutes or until golden. Serve warm on its own or with a spoonful of whole-egg custard.

* Suitable for freezing

Baby's serve: This does have a little added sugar so you might like to wait until your baby is a bit older before serving it to him. However, a small serving as an occasional treat, with some custard stirred through, is a nice way to include him in family mealtimes — and at least the sugar comes packaged with all the goodness of the nutrient-rich apples, berries and oats. You can blend or mash it to the right consistency.

Toddler's serve: Simply serve as is with some whole-egg custard.

CHEAT'S BANANA ICE CREAM

SERVES 4

• • • • • • • • • • • • • • • • • • • •

No ice cream machine is needed for this delicious dessert. And it's lovely to know that giving your child healthy, home-made foods doesn't mean depriving her of an ice creamy treat.

3 bananas, peeled
185 ml (6 fl oz/¾ cup) coconut cream
2–3 tablespoons maple syrup

Break the bananas into large chunks, place in a container and freeze for 3 hours. Meanwhile, place the coconut cream in the refrigerator to chill.

Blend the frozen banana with the coconut cream and maple syrup until smooth and creamy. Serve immediately or return to the freezer for about 30 minutes to firm up before serving.

> **Baby's serve:** Most babies don't like ice cream as they find it too cold. However, your baby might like a try. Because there is a little added sweetness, don't serve her too much.
>
> **Toddler's serve:** To make your toddler's serving extra special, top with some finely chopped nuts and fresh berries or blueberry sauce (page 145). If it's a special occasion, you could drizzle over a little melted chocolate instead.

CREAMY COUSCOUS PUDDING

SERVES 3–4

• • • • • • • • • • • • • • • • • • • •

If rice pudding is a hit in your house, try this quick and delicious variation using couscous.

375 ml (12½ fl oz/1½ cups) milk
95 g (3 oz/½ cup) instant couscous
2 tablespoons maple syrup or soft brown sugar
2 tablespoons raisins or sultanas (golden raisins)
1 tablespoon chopped dried apricots
1 tablespoon plain yoghurt
¼ teaspoon vanilla extract
¼ teaspoon ground cinnamon

Heat the milk in a saucepan until it has just reached scalding (almost boiling) point. Remove from the heat and stir through all of the remaining ingredients.

Cover and stand for 20 minutes or until the couscous has absorbed the milk. Serve warm.

> **Baby's serve:** Because this dish has added sugar, just give your baby a small taste. You may like to chop up the raisins and stir through some more yoghurt.
>
> **Toddler's serve:** Serve as is.

WHOLE-EGG CUSTARD

MAKES ABOUT 2 CUPS

The ultimate comfort food, this custard is delicious with fruit crumble, or with some sliced banana or fresh berries. It's half as sweet as a traditional custard recipe, making it healthier for your baby and toddler. It also uses the whole egg, rather than just the yolk, for a lighter, no-waste custard.

500 ml (17 fl oz/2 cups) milk
½ teaspoon vanilla extract
3 eggs
1 tablespoon soft brown or white sugar
1 tablespoon cornflour (cornstarch)

Baby's serve: Make this a nutritious dessert for your baby by stirring a small spoonful through a serving of fresh fruit purée as a little treat.

Toddler's serve: Serve as is with sliced fresh fruit.

Heat the milk and vanilla in a small saucepan until it is just starting to bubble.

Meanwhile, using a hand-held whisk, whisk the eggs, sugar and cornflour in a large bowl until well combined.

Slowly pour the milk mixture over the egg mixture, whisking continuously until combined. Return the mixture to the saucepan and cook, stirring, over low heat until the mixture thickens and coats the back of a spoon. Remove from the heat, cover the surface with plastic wrap (cling film) to prevent a skin from forming, and set aside to cool to the desired temperature.

Variation: To make a quick rice custard, you can stir some cooked rice through your toddler's serve of custard, or for a smoother texture, use rice cereal.

VANILLA RISOTTO PUDDING

SERVES 4–6

I think this sweet, creamy risotto is even more delicious than an oven-baked rice pudding. If I've been organised enough to make my favourite fruit compote, I serve them together.

1 litre (34 fl oz/4 cups) milk
110 g (4 oz/½ cup) arborio rice
2 tablespoons sugar
1 teaspoon vanilla extract
Vanilla fruit compote (page 91) and ground cinnamon, to serve (optional)

> **Baby's serve:** Because this dish has a little added sugar, give your baby just a small taste. Alternatively, you can set aside your baby's serving before stirring in the sugar. You'll probably need to spoonfeed your baby this dish, as it will be a bit tricky for him to eat with his hands.
>
> **Toddler's serve:** Although this dish has some sweetness, it has far less than most desserts. Chop up the fruit compote (if you've made this too) and stir it through your toddler's serving.

Heat the milk in a saucepan until it has just reached scalding (almost boiling) point. Reduce the heat to a gentle simmer. Add the rice and cook over low–medium heat, stirring frequently, for 25 minutes or until the milk has been absorbed and the rice is creamy and tender.

Stir in the sugar and vanilla until well combined. Serve with the vanilla fruit compote and a sprinkle of cinnamon on top.

MANGO TAPIOCA PUDDINGS

SERVES 6

• ı •

This is an easy-peasy dessert: soft and light, and perfect served with a little yoghurt or cream on a hot summer's evening. The mango is a refreshing take on the traditional lemon tapioca pudding.

145 g (5 oz/¾ cup) seed tapioca
1 quantity Mango purée (page 71)
2 tablespoons sugar (optional)
3 tablespoons plain yoghurt

> **Baby's serve:** This dessert is delicious without any sugar because of the natural sweetness of the mango. But, if you like, you can make baby's serve and then stir through some sugar for the rest of the family. A younger baby may find it a bit lumpy (in which case you could blend it), but she should be fine with it by seven or eight months.
>
> **Toddler's serve:** Serve as is.

Bring 2 litres (68 fl oz/8 cups) water to the boil in a large saucepan over high heat. Reduce the heat to medium and gradually add the tapioca, stirring constantly. Simmer for 15 minutes or until the tapioca is transparent. (Check the transparency by removing a couple of balls from the water and holding them up to the light. When ready, the tapioca will have changed from opaque to transparent.)

Drain the tapioca in a sieve and rinse under cold water until it is clear. Transfer to a large bowl and combine with the mango purée and sugar.

Divide the tapioca mixture among six small glasses or ramekins. Cover with plastic wrap (cling film) and chill for 45 minutes or until firm.

Serve chilled or at room temperature, topped with a dollop of yoghurt.

INDEX

Page numbers in *italics* indicate recipes.

Published in 2012 by Hardie Grant Books

Hardie Grant Books (Australia)
Ground Floor, Building 1
658 Church Street
Richmond, Victoria 3121
www.hardiegrant.com.au

Hardie Grant Books (UK)
Dudley House, North Suite
34–35 Southampton Street
London WC2E 7HF
www.hardiegrant.co.uk

Cataloguing-in-Publication data is available from the
National Library of Australia.
Cooking For Your Baby and Toddler
ISBN 9781742701363

Publishing Director: Paul McNally
Managing Editor: Gordana Trifunovic
Project Editor: Lucy Heaver
Editor: Justine Harding
Design Manager: Heather Menzies
Concept Designer: Alex Frampton
Typesetter: Megan Ellis
Photographer: Ben Dearnley
Stylist: Michelle Noerianto
Production: Penny Sanderson

Colour reproduction by Splitting Image Colour Studio
Printed in China by 1010 Printing International Limited

Recipes were tested using a 20 ml tablespoon. All recipes
use free-range eggs, chicken, bacon and ham.

Every effort has been made to ensure that the information
presented in this book is complete and accurate. The ideas
and suggestions contained in the book are not intended as a
substitute for consultation with your healthcare provider. All
matters regarding the health of you and your child must be
supervised by a medical professional. Neither the publisher
nor the author accept any legal responsibility for any personal
injury or other damage or loss arising from the use or misuse
of the information and advice in this book.

Many thanks for the generous loan of props for the
photography go to Sunbeam, Maxwell Williams,
Robert Gordon Australia, Mud Australia and Funkis.